Value for Money

Executive Compensation in the 1990s

Edward Iacobucci

with Michael J. Trebilcock

with comments by
James C. Baillie, Austin C. Beutel, Robert D. Brown,
Martin F. Harts, Thomas E. Kierans, Donald P. Lewis,
Jeffrey G. MacIntosh, John D. McNeil, Randall K. Morck,
Edward J. Waitzer, and Adam H. Zimmerman

Observation 41

C.D. Howe Institute

C.D. Howe Institute publications are available from:
Renouf Publishing Company Limited, 1294 Algoma Road,
Ottawa, Ontario K1B 3W8; phone (613) 741-4333; fax (613) 741-5439

and from Renouf's stores at:
71½ Sparks Street, Ottawa (613) 238-8985
12 Adelaide Street West, Toronto (416) 363-3171

For trade book orders, please contact:
McGraw-Hill Ryerson Limited, 300 Water Street,
Whitby, Ontario L1N 9B6; phone (416) 430-5050

For college book orders, please contact:
Prentice-Hall Canada Inc., 1870 Birchmount Road,
Scarborough, Ontario M1P 2J7; phone (416) 293-3621

Institute publications are also available in microform from:
Micromedia Limited, 20 Victoria Street,
Toronto, Ontario M5C 2N8

This book is printed on recycled, acid-free paper.

Canadian Cataloguing in Publication Data

Iacobucci, Edward
Value for money : executive compensation in the 1990s

(Observation, ISSN 0826-9947 ; 41)
Includes bibliographical references.
ISBN 0-88806-393-8

1. Executives – Salaries, etc. – Canada. I. Trebilcock,
Michael J., 1941– . II. Baillie, James C.
III. C.D. Howe Institute. IV. Title. V. Series:
Observation (C.D. Howe Institute). English ; 41.

HD4965.C2I2 1996 331.2'816584'00971 C96-931236-9

Cover design by Leroux Design Inc.
Printed in Canada by Kromar Printing Ltd.,
Winnipeg, Manitoba, August 1996.

Contents

Foreword

This monograph evolved out of a Roundtable on Executive Compensation jointly sponsored by the C.D. Howe Institute, the Ontario Securities Commission, and the Law and Economics Programme at the University of Toronto, and held at the C.D. Howe Institute on December 15, 1995. The roundtable was conceived of by Michael J. Trebilcock, Director of the Law and Economics Programme at the University of Toronto; Edward J. Waitzer, Chairman of the Ontario Securities Commission; and me. We did so in recognition of the high public profile that executive compensation issues have attracted in the press and other media, and the controversies and debates these issues have provoked in both scholarly and popular writing. In hard economic times, workers facing pressures on wages and benefits and reduced job security are often surprised, and sometimes indignant, at the levels of compensation that corporations pay their senior executives.

The roundtable was organized around an overview paper prepared by Edward Iacobucci, a recent graduate of the University of Toronto Law School, which reviewed both the theoretical literature on the incentive properties of alternative compensation regimes for corporate executives and the empirical evidence as to whether these regimes in fact serve socially productive purposes. Discussants were then asked to prepare written comments reacting to the arguments and empirical evidence reviewed in the overview paper and addressing the following three themes:

- Is there a problem with executive compensation?
- If there is a problem, what are its causes?
- If there is a problem and if its causes can be identified, what policy responses are appropriate?

At the roundtable, discussion sessions were organized around each of these themes and this book, which was edited by Michael J.

Trebilcock, largely follows the same organization — that is, the main paper is followed by discussants' comments grouped loosely around the three themes, although many of the discussants address more than one theme.

I believe readers will find that the overview paper and the discussants' comments provide a full and balanced ventilation of most of the important features of the debate on executive compensation.

The volume was copy edited by Lenore d'Anjou and Barry A. Norris, and prepared for publication by Wendy Longsworth. The analysis and opinions presented in the study are the responsibility of the authors, and do not necessarily reflect the views of the members or Board of Directors of the C.D. Howe Institute.

Thomas E. Kierans
President and
Chief Executive Officer

The Law and Economics of Executive Compensation

Edward Iacobucci

with Michael J. Trebilcock

In 1982, *Fortune* magazine published an article, provocatively entitled "The Madness of Executive Compensation," that noted the high salaries and bonuses of various corporate executives in the United States, including Rand Araskog, chairman of ITT, who had received compensation of $1.15 million in 1981 (Loomis 1982, 42). If this amount constituted "madness," one would be hard pressed to describe the compensation of that country's chief executive officers (CEOs) and other top executives less than a decade later. *Business Week* (Byrne 1991, 90) reports that, in 1986, Lee Iacocca of Chrysler earned a then-unprecedented compensation package of $20.5 million; a year later, Charles Lazarus, chairman of Toys 'R' Us, took home more than $60 million; in 1988, Michael Eisner of Disney earned $40.1 million for his efforts; and in 1990, Time Warner's Steven J. Ross realized $78.2 million and Donald Pels, the chief executive of LIN Broadcasting, earned $186.2 million. Finally, in 1993, Disney rewarded Eisner with the sum of $203.0 million (Hardy 1994, 141).

Canadian executives generally lag behind their colleagues to the south in compensation, but several are doing very well. In 1991, Peter Munk, chairman of American Barrick Resources, reaped a then-unprecedented $32.3 million, but this record was broken in 1993 by Frank Stronach's pay package of almost $41 million, earned as chairman of Magna International (Pritchard 1994, B1).

These staggering figures have created a great deal of controversy and inspired diametrically opposed opinions. Compare the titles of two well-known commentaries on executive compensation: "Top Executives Are Worth Every Nickel They Get" (Murphy 1986), and *In Search of Excess: The Overcompensation of American Executives* (Crystal 1991b). This paper sketches the contours of the debate, primarily by means of a literature review.

I begin by outlining the economic theory of compensation for labor and the basic reasons behind various executive compensation schemes. Then, I present the empirical evidence on compensation, outline the legal framework for establishing executive compensation packages, and explain how this framework could lead to inappropriate compensation schemes. Finally, I survey proposed reforms to the existing compensation decision process and suggest some areas for further study.

The Economics of Executive Compensation

In a perfectly competitive labor market, say the economists, each worker is willing to work for a wage no lower than he could obtain in alternative employment. Each employer, on the other hand, pays whatever wage is necessary to hire an additional worker so long as hiring him is profitable. As a result, the worker is paid his value to the firm: the value of the marginal product of his labor.[1] If this theoretical process accurately described what happens in the market for executives, there should be little controversy over their pay. Each would receive the value of his marginal product. This story, however, is far too simplistic to describe compensation in the executive labor market; it does not reflect the divergence of interests between the owners of a corporation and the managers who control it. Because of this divergence, how executives are paid influences their marginal products (see Jensen and Murphy 1990a). Compensation itself alters productivity.

1 For more elaboration on the theory of the determination of wages, see Gunderson (1993).

The Separation of Ownership and Control

In most major corporations in today's economy, shareholders are the firm's owners, but rarely are they its managers. This split has long been recognized as creating an inefficient divergence between the owners' and the managers' motivations. While owners are said to care only about profit, managers may not face the proper incentives to maximize it. Indeed, this potential for inefficiency was noted by Adam Smith:

> The directors of such [joint-stock] companies, however, being the managers rather of other people's money than of their own, it cannot well be expected, that they should watch over it with the same anxious vigilance with which the partners in a private copartner frequently watch over their own. Like the stewards of a rich man, they are apt to consider attention to small matters as not for their master's honor, and very easily give themselves a dispensation from having it. Negligence and profusion, therefore, must always prevail, more or less, in the management of the affairs of such a company. ([1776] 1937, 700.)

In the first half of this century, Berle and Means explored the economic implications of the trend toward increased public ownership of corporations. They were pessimistic:

> Though the American law makes no distinction between the private corporation and the quasi-public, the economics of the two are essentially different. The separation of ownership from control produces a condition where the interests of owner and ultimate manager may, and often do, diverge....Those who control the destinies of the typical modern corporation own so insignificant a fraction of the company's stock that the returns from running the corporation profitably accrue to them in only a very minor degree. The stockholders, on the other hand, to whom the profits of the corporation go, cannot be motivated by those profits to a more efficient use of the property, since they have surrendered all disposition of it to those in control of the enterprise. The explosion of the atom of property destroys the basis of the old assumption that the quest for profits will spur the owner of industrial property to its effective use. (1933, 7–9.)

More recently, Jensen and Meckling have examined the implications of the separation of ownership and control for a firm's optimal capital structure. As a preliminary observation, they note:

> While the literature of economics is replete with references to the "theory of the firm", the material generally subsumed under that heading is not a theory of the firm, but actually a theory of markets in which firms are important actors. The firm is a "black box" operated so as to meet the relevant marginal conditions with respect to inputs and outputs, thereby maximizing profits, or more accurately, present value. Except for a few recent and tentative steps, however, we have no theory which explains how the conflicting objectives of the individual participants are brought into equilibrium so as to yield this result. (1976, 306–307.)

Focusing on the implications for the motivation of managers of owning a smaller proportion of the firm's capital, Jensen and Meckling note that one result is significant agency costs, which they define as the costs a principal faces as a consequence of suboptimal behavior associated with outside capital. As the proportion of equity held by the manager falls, so does the cost *to her* of indulging in suboptimal activities, such as illicit perquisite consumption. The authors conclude that outside share ownership increases these agency costs.[2] In contrast, as Fama notes, when the manager is the firm's sole security holder,

> there is clearly no incentive problem. When he is sole security holder, a manager consumes on the job, through shirking, perquisites, or incompetence, to the point where these yield marginal expected utility equal to that provided by an additional dollar of wealth usable for consumption or investment outside of the firm. (1980, 295.)

Various institutions are identified as providing discipline for corporate managers. As Trebilcock summarizes:

2 For further exploration of this theme, see Fama (1980); and Fama and Jensen (1983).

> The recent literature identifies three main factors that help align the interests of principals and agents in publicly traded corporations: the market for managers, the output market and the market for corporate control. First, competition in the market among and for managers encourages greater efficiency, greater innovation, and lower agency costs. Second, competition among firms in their output markets requires firms to act efficiently if they are to survive and if managers are to retain their jobs. Third, private capital markets where firms must raise equity or debt capital will discipline weak management....In addition, where a firm's shares are traded on the stock market, corporate takeovers are possible whenever a company is being poorly managed. (1994, 9–10.)

Agency Costs

Although these institutions are indeed significant in controlling agency costs, a manager's compensation scheme may also serve as a control. Before considering this potential role of compensation schemes, it is useful to outline the types of agency problems that may arise. They can be grouped under two broad headings: overconsumption of perquisites, and suboptimal choices about risk.

Perquisites

Perquisite overconsumption can take a variety of forms. An executive may use the firm's resources for his own private benefit by endowing himself with items such as lavish office furniture or private jets. Some of the most notorious examples of this form of agency cost were provided by the executives at RJR Nabisco before its takeover by Kohlberg, Kravis and Roberts. Consider the following description of executive headquarters:

> The reception area's backdrop was an eighteenth-century $100,000 lacquered Chinese screen, complemented by a $16,000 pair of powder blue Chinese vases from a slightly later dynasty. Visitors could settle into a set of French Empire mahogany chairs ($30,000) and ogle the two matching *bibliothèque* cabinets ($30,000) from the same period. In each was an English porcelain dessert service in a tobacco-leaf pattern ($20,000). (Burroughs and Helyar 1990, 93.)

Perquisite overconsumption may also take the form of enjoying too much leisure time or of empire building. Rather than providing full effort, an executive may prefer to shirk on the job, providing herself with a good, leisure, but depriving the firm of value. A potentially devastating incentive is the pleasure an executive may derive from becoming a "captain of industry" at the helm of a mighty conglomerate, which may lead to the costly, inefficient acquisition of other firms.

To illustrate how such agency costs are aggravated by increasing outside capital, consider the following simple numerical example. Suppose an hour of shirking brings the executive a private benefit of $3.00, but reduces his productivity to the firm by $4.00. If the manager is the firm's sole owner, shirking will cost him $4.00 but will bring him only a $3.00 benefit, so he will not shirk. If, however, he owns only half the firm, shirking will personally cost him only $2.00, so he may shirk.

Risk

A second type of agency cost concerns risk. Shareholders diversify their portfolios so as to minimize risk to themselves. Consequently, they are approximately risk neutral with respect to the actions of a particular firm. No matter what the riskiness (variance) of the payoffs from a particular course of action, shareholders prefer that managers pursue projects with the highest expected values. Managers, however, may not be risk neutral with respect to investment decisions. For example, since their reputations in the managerial labor market are affected by the outcome of the investment decisions they make and since they are unable to diversify their investment in reputation, they will likely display some risk aversion in making these decisions. As a result, they may pursue not profit-maximizing courses of action but rather courses that maximize their personal utility, which may not include risky ventures.[3]

3 For a seminal discussion of the effects of risk aversion on incentive schemes, see Holmstrom (1979).

For an illustration of this agency cost, consider another simple numerical example. The manager faces a choice between two investments. Investment A has a guaranteed profit of $1.00 to the firm, which will preserve the manager's reputation for sound investment. Investment B has a 50 percent chance of utter failure and a profit of nil, and a 50 percent chance of success and a profit of $3.00. If the project fails, the manager's reputation will be significantly harmed, thus lowering her expected future wages, but if the project pays off, her reputation will be enhanced, thus increasing her future expected wages. Shareholders, being risk neutral, prefer investment B, which has an expected profit of $1.50, to investment A, with an expected payoff of only $1.00. A risk-averse manager, however, may choose investment A, which guarantees the preservation of her reputation, rather than investment B, which puts her reputation at risk.

Risk aversion may thus lead to further agency costs as the result of the separation of ownership and control.

Executive Compensation and Agency Costs

If shareholders and executives could enter into fully contingent claims contracts, agency costs could be eliminated by contract. That is, as Jensen and Murphy say,

> [i]f shareholders had complete information regarding the CEO's activities and the firm's investment opportunities, they could design a contract specifying and enforcing the managerial action to be taken in each state of the world. (1990b, 226.)

In this case, agency costs would be eliminated simply by penalizing the CEO for breaching this complete contract.

Of course, such a suggestion is hardly practical. As the authors continue,

> [m]anagerial actions and investment opportunities are not, however, perfectly observable by shareholders; indeed, shareholders

> do not often know what actions the CEO *can* take or which of these actions will increase shareholder wealth. (Ibid.)

This is not to say that contractual arrangements are unable to address these problems. Although it would be impractical to incorporate explicit instructions about perks and risks in an executive's contract, such a contract can include incentives that make it in the executive's best interests to promote the owners' goal of profit maximization. Properly framed compensation arrangements may better motivate an executive, reducing agency costs. As Lambert and Larcker put it:

> "[A]gency theory" has focused attention on the separation of ownership from control in large public corporations. In the context of this theory, management incentive compensation plans are viewed as one of several important means of reducing potential conflicts of interest between management and shareholders....To the extent that the separation of ownership from control is a serious problem in the large public corporation..., an effective compensation program can add value to the firm by improving the alignment of management incentives with stockholder interests. (1991, 100.)

In the numerical examples above, the agency costs resulted because the private benefit to the executive from engaging in suboptimal activity was greater than the private cost, even though the social benefit of optimal behavior was greater than the social cost. A properly framed compensation contract can lower the private benefit of engaging in a particular undesirable activity, increase the private benefit of engaging in desirable activities, and/or increase the cost to the executive of engaging in suboptimal behavior.

The following discussion outlines the basic forms of executive compensation[4] and the type of agency cost each scheme may address.[5]

4 The forms of compensation considered here are those outlined in Milgrom and Roberts (1992, 425).

5 To focus the discussion on the effect of compensation schemes, I assume throughout that outside discipline on managerial behavior — such as an executive's desire to protect his reputation in the managerial labor market — is of trivial importance; the executive's incentives depend on the compensation scheme.

Bonuses

Milgrom and Roberts define a *bonus* as

> [a] nominally variable amount, often paid as a lump sum, at the discretion of the firm's directors. May be tied to performance either implicitly or through an explicit formula. If so, performance is usually measured on a short-term basis, such as the previous year's accounting profits or earnings growth, or the extent to which these exceed targets. (1992, 425.)

The implicit or explicit promise of a bonus for observed levels of his firm's performance provides the executive with a private incentive to ensure that it performs well. Consider the simple numerical example of the executive to whom the cost of working an additional hour was $3.00, but the benefit to the firm was $4.00. If his pay is constructed so that he receives a bonus of $3.50 for generating an extra $4.00, he will not shirk and there is a Pareto improvement over the no-bonus situation: the executive is better off by $0.50 ($3.50 bonus less $3.00 cost of effort) and the firm is also better off by $0.50 ($4.00 worth of effort less $3.50 bonus). Bonuses thus attenuate the agency cost of shirking (or, more generally, perquisite consumption).

Firms use a variety of types of bonus systems. A common mechanism is to reward executives by paying them a bonus whose size depends on the firm's return on equity (ROE). This relationship may be linear (for every percentage point that the ROE increases, the executive's pay increases) or nonlinear (for every percentage point above a certain minimum ROE, the executive's pay increases).

The latter system was the one implemented by Disney when it hired Michael Eisner. Crystal (1991a, 353–355) reports that, at the time (1984), Disney was a mediocre performer, earning about a 9 percent ROE. Eisner's compensation package for each of the six years of the contract included a base salary of $750,000 (which was low for a CEO in the major entertainment industry) and an annual bonus equal to 2 percent of all after-tax profits in excess of a 9 percent ROE. Disney's performance improved dramatically. In 1983, its profit was in the $100 million range; by 1988, it had risen to $550 million. The stock price was about $14 a share when Eisner joined the firm; by 1988, it had risen to $66. Eisner's compensation reflected this growth in prosperity, with his annual bonus reaching the $7 million level. On its face, the compensation package offered Eisner appears to have provided him with incentives that were desirable from a shareholder perspective; Crystal estimates that Disney's performance outstripped by around $5 billion what the author deems appropriate expectations for growth in shareholder wealth.

Other measures for determining executives' annual bonus include annual profit (either before tax or net of tax), earnings per share, and growth in earnings per share. In all these cases, the bonus is usually based on the amount by which the firm's performance exceeds a specified level of the chosen statistic.

Drawbacks. Bonuses may be valuable tools in the hands of the principals (the shareholders) to induce desirable activity from their agents (the executives). They may, however, also have significant drawbacks both for shareholders and for executives.

First, they may induce incorrect incentives with respect to the horizon of executive decisionmaking. Shareholder (and societal) value is maximized by choosing investments that have a positive net present value to the firm. If, however, the profit from a particular project is in the relatively distant future, an executive whose discount rate is higher than that of the firm (perhaps because her retirement is imminent) may choose to pursue alternative projects with expected profit that is low overall, but high in the immediate future. Bonuses thus may encourage executive myopia. As Burchman says:

> [A]nnual earnings do not capture the future impact of current decisions on earnings. For example, while major investments in advertising and research and development may have an immediate depressing effect on earnings, they may have a significant long-term positive effect on future earnings. (1991, 197.)

Second, earnings measures may not accurately reflect the performance of the executive herself but exogenous factors that are internal or external to the firm. Internally, there is little doubt that, although a CEO is an important determinant of a firm's performance, its other employees can have a critical effect on profit. For example, a breakthrough (or setback) in research and development may significantly affect earnings, and therefore executive pay, with little connection to executive performance. Externally, poor or admirable firm performance may depend on industry trends that are also unconnected to executive performance. No matter how diligent the CEO, an increase in the cost of inputs resulting from, say, a natural disaster will reduce profit.

The imperfect correlation between executive effort and firm performance results in unwanted risk to the managers, who, unlike shareholders, are unable to diversify their earnings "portfolio." As Daniels puts it:

> Because the value of managerial performance is not perfectly observable, shareholders must rely on proxy measurements.... In some cases, however, these measurements, while bearing rough correspondence to managerial effort, incorporate factors that are beyond the control of managers. This, in turn, imposes non-diversifiable risks on managers. (1994, 43.)

This risk has essentially two related costs, as Lambert and Larcker point out:

> First, an increase in management's exposure to risk will make the compensation scheme less attractive, all other things being equal; and in return for bearing additional risk, executives collectively will require an increase in the general level of their compensation. Second, increasing an executive's exposure to risk may cause him to become more conservative in his investment strategy. An executive may turn down risky projects and accept only "safe" projects offering sizable, but substandard returns. (1991, 103.)

The advantages of portfolio diversification, which allows shareholders to be risk neutral with respect to the performance of a particular firm, are undermined if the manager of each firm is risk averse and faces risk in his compensation package. Rather than choosing projects that maximize expected profit, managers may choose investments with smaller but more certain returns.

Risk Reduction. Comparative performance measures may usefully reduce the risk a manager faces from industry trends. If the industry has slumped generally, a relative performance measure captures that effect, and the manager is not necessarily penalized personally for an industry trend. In contrast, poor performance relative to other firms in the industry is likely related to firm-specific factors, and the manager is appropriately penalized. As Lambert and Larcker say:

> In such *relative* performance schemes, executive compensation is set according to how well the company performs relative to a comparison or peer group. The implicit assumption underlying this approach is that the construction of a peer group allows general market or macroeconomic influences and industry-specific influences to be removed from the performance measure, thereby providing a better measure of an executive's distinctive contribution to the firm's profitability. (Ibid., 104.)

As Holmstrom (1979) shows, the increased accuracy of a performance proxy reduces the risk facing managers, which, in turn, allows the firm to lower the level of compensation while leaving managers' utility unchanged. Furthermore, the cost of risk-averse decisionmaking on the part of executives is reduced.

Summary. In sum, bonuses provide executives with incentives that can control agency costs, but they have disadvantages such as encouraging managerial myopia and increasing managerial risk. This risk may be reduced, however, by basing the bonus on relative measures, rather than strictly on firm-specific measures.

Salaries

Milgrom and Roberts define *salary* as

> [a]n amount paid over the course of the year and fixed in advance. Salary may be adjusted regularly based on length of service, competitive conditions, the cost of living, performance, or other considerations. (1992, 425.)

Unlike a bonus, an annual salary is not contingent on the firm's performance for that year. Its central advantage to both the manager and the firm's owners is its risk-reducing qualities. Since the salary is fixed, the manager's actions have no immediate impact on his remuneration. The desirable effects are twofold. First, with the cost of risk to the manager reduced, his level of compensation may be lower than in a riskier pay structure yet leave him just as well off. Thus, the amount of compensation is generally lower if paid as salary than if paid as a bonus, which, *ceteris paribus*, leaves the manager equally well off and the shareholders better off. As Milgrom and Roberts state:

> If the firm can be treated as risk neutral (perhaps because it is owned by investors with well-diversified portfolios), then, other things being equal, it should seek to insulate the workers fully against income risk. This provides a value-creating service for the employees while imposing no cost or risk premium on the risk-neutral firm. The expected pay level can be reduced without harming the workers if the firm takes on some of the risk they would otherwise face, and so both sides can gain. (1992, 333.)

A second effect of the risk-reducing qualities of a fixed salary is the corresponding reduction in the risk aversion of managers in choosing investment opportunities. Recall the example in which the manager must choose investment A with a guaranteed payoff of \$1.00, or investment B with a 50 percent chance of no payoff and a 50 percent chance of a payoff of \$3.00. If remuneration depends on the payoff from the investment, a risk-averse manager is more likely to choose the guaranteed return offered by investment A, contrary to the wishes of shareholders. If, however, she is secure in receiving her salary regardless of the outcome of the investment, she is more likely to choose the profit-maximizing course of investment B. A salary thus serves to mitigate the agency costs associated with risk-averse managers.

Drawbacks. The disadvantages of a fixed salary reflect the principal-agent problems already discussed. Since a manager on fixed salary faces no gain or loss from either providing optimal effort or engaging in suboptimal activities such as perquisite consumption, the likelihood of the latter increases. An executive who is paid strictly by salary is more likely to shirk and to consume other perks rather than to engage in utility-reducing hard work. In other words, although a fixed salary may induce an executive to take a lower salary to engage in riskier investments, it provides little in the way of incentive to add value to the firm. The insurance-enhancing properties of a salary must be balanced against its inability to control moral hazard.

Summary. In sum, tension exists between bonus and salary as tools for compensation. A bonus helps align executive and shareholder interests with respect to perquisite consumption but exposes the manager to unwanted risk; a fixed salary, on the other hand, insulates the executive from risk but fails to discourage moral hazard. As Milgrom and Roberts say, the goals of compensation policy "may not be consistent. For example,...providing motivation may require basing pay on performance. However, this may prevent realizing the gains that would come from insulating employees against income risk" (ibid., 390).

Stock Awards

Milgrom and Roberts define *stock awards* as

> [s]hares in the firm given to the executive or sold to him or her at a deep discount. Often the ability of the executive to sell this stock is restricted, at least until certain conditions are met. (Ibid., 425.)

The main strength of this form of compensation, it is said, is that it aligns the interests of the executive with those of the shareholders. Any increase in the value of the stock will lead to an increase in the executive's private wealth, thereby inducing him to maximize shareholder wealth. As Buyniski states:

> Perhaps the prime reason why stock compensation is still appropriate is that none of the alternatives provide the same or similar benefits in an efficient manner. Specifically, nonstock vehicles cannot directly tie executive returns to shareholder wealth. (1991, 306.)

Or as Milgrom and Roberts put it:

> [A]ssuming that the market value of the firm at any point reflects the best estimate of the future cash flows that the firm will generate, market-value maximization is again the proper test of performance. Tying the CEO's pay to the value of the firm would direct attention exactly where it belongs. (1992, 437.)

Drawbacks. The drawback of stock grants is similar to the problem with bonuses: although they help to align the interests of managers and shareholders with respect to value maximization, they are risky for the executive. Undertaking a successful project may increase the value of the shares and thus increase the executive's compensation, but undertaking a failed project may lower it. A privately risk-averse manager may therefore choose investments that are safe rather than those that are value maximizing. Stock awards thus provide incentives for value maximization that may be attenuated by managerial risk aversion.

Stock Options

As defined by Milgrom and Roberts, *stock options* are

> [r]ights given to the executive to buy stock in the firm at a prespecified price during a specific period of time. The price is usually at or above the current price of the stock when the

> options are awarded, and the time period is usually several years. No actual cash is received until the executive actually buys the stock. Then the compensation is the difference between the market price of the stock and the exercise price (the amount paid by the executive). (Ibid., 425.)

This form of compensation is the most frequently used of the various stock compensation schemes; in 1987, 81 percent of companies in the United States that used stock compensation used options (Buyniski 1991, 291).

The popularity of options has a variety of reasons. First, they accomplish the basic task of aligning manager and shareholder interests. For an executive to reap any benefit from holding the option, the value of the firm's stock must rise above the strike price (the prespecified price of the option). Thus, the executive has an incentive to increase the value of the firm. Options do not, however, expose managers to as significant a risk as compensation schemes, such as bonuses and stock awards, in which pay is explicitly lowered by poor performance. Milgrom and Roberts observe that the tradeoff between incentives and insurance implies that owners should

> [g]ive as much insurance as possible, which basically means reward people for success and try not to have them bear the costs of failures. Note that charging them for failures would accentuate the risk they already face [from managerial labor markets and the value of their human capital] and make them even more reluctant to recommend projects.
>
> Giving stock options to managers has this effect because successes are rewarded and there is no direct cost to failures. (1992, 431.)

In other words, the executive's possible gain from a successful project that increases the value of her options may outweigh the cost of potentially forgone gains. Managers may therefore be induced to choose riskier, profit-maximizing investments rather than safer, sub-profit-maximizing investments.[6]

6 Indeed, options may induce managers to indulge in excessively risky investment, as discussed below.

Another reason for the popularity of options results from current accounting principles. Although the Financial Accounting Standards Board in the United States has tightened some of the rules regarding the accounting treatment of stock compensation, anomalies remain. One is that the granting of stock options involves no accounting charges; boards may issue options to executives without incurring a bottom-line cost. This situation has led, some commentators suggest, to the excessive use of options as a compensation tool. Crystal states:

> [I]f you don't charge earnings for the cost of providing an economic benefit...you are likely to start thinking that benefit has no cost at all. And like any underpriced resource, you start to hand out too much of it. (1991b, 233.)

One cost of the overuse of options is the dilution of the value of shares held by other investors in the company. In Canada, this concern recently increased with the Toronto Stock Exchange's (TSE's) removal of its previous 10 percent limit on incentive shares (see Mackenzie 1995).

A further problem with options is their grantors' lack of commitment to a particular strike price. Crystal (1991b, 175–176) suggests that "an increasing number of boards are wont" to lower the strike price if the share price of the company falls dramatically. For example, he says, Frank Lorenzo of Texas Air held options with a strike price of $30.00 per share; when the share price collapsed, they were transformed into options with a strike price of only $4.625 per share. If boards cannot credibly commit to maintaining the specified strike price, the incentive to increase the value of the shares may be attenuated. If the stock performs poorly, the executive may simply lobby the board for a lower strike price.

Drawbacks. Because stock options reward an executive's success and do not penalize his failures with out-of-pocket costs, they may work too well, reducing risk aversion to an excessive degree. As Loomis states:

> In a totally rational world, top executives would get paid handsomely for first-class performance, and would lose out when they flopped. But to an extraordinary extent, those who flop still get paid handsomely. (1982, 42.)

Many commentators suggest that options fail to penalize flopping sufficiently and thus fail to provide executives with proper incentives. One manifestation of this failure is executives' assumption of risk that is excessive from the firm's point of view but not their own. If the gamble pays off, they will reap enormous windfalls from their options; if it does not, they will not suffer any out-of-pocket costs. One commentator puts the situation this way:

> There is a crisis in executive compensation, but the critics are looking at the wrong crisis.
>
> Most people think the problem is with compensation *levels.* They think American corporations pay their executives too much....But that is not the real crisis in executive compensation....The problem is the particular executive behavior that too many compensation plans motivate. Stock option plans specifically motivate executives to take strategic risks — often in the form of acquisitions — that are more hazardous than the shareholders desire. (Kay 1992, 1.)

Thus, options may be so successful in reducing risk to managers that agency costs may result.

Stock Appreciation Rights and Phantom Shares

In order to redress the dilution problem associated with stock awards and stock options, some firms have developed stock appreciation rights (SARs) and phantom shares. Milgrom and Roberts define *SARs* as

> [r]ights to collect the amount of any share price appreciation on a specified amount of common stock over time. (1992, 425.)

Thus, SARs align the interests of shareholders and executives insofar as they, like stock awards, induce the executive to maximize shareholder value. The dilution of existing shares, however, is eliminated since no new shares are actually issued.

Phantom shares act even more like an actual share award. Milgrom and Roberts define them as

> [u]nits that correspond to common stock but carry no ownership claims. These entitle the executive to receive the share price appreciation and dividends that would have been received on actual stock. (Ibid.)

Thus, phantom shares also provide executives with incentives similar to those of a stock award but avoid a dilution problem.

Compensation Levels

Thus far, the discussion has ignored the optimal amount or level of compensation. To address this issue, consider first the simplest explanation of compensation levels. Each worker is willing to accept a particular compensation scheme only if no other firm will offer her more; each firm is willing to compensate a worker up to the point at which it is no longer profitable to hire her at this level of compensation. Consequently, each worker will be paid the value of the marginal product of her labor. If executive compensation were governed by this algorithm, executives would be compensated (on average) at levels that corresponded to their marginal product.

Although paying executives the value of their marginal product may result in very high salaries (it is difficult to determine what executives' marginal product is), a different theory suggests that it may be appropriate to pay the CEO and other top executives explicitly more than their marginal product. Lazear and Rosen (1981) suggest that paying more than the marginal product to the winners of a competition may induce optimal behavior from all participants. If the prize at the top is sufficiently enticing, lower-level employees will compete for promotion, providing the firm with more productive labor at lower levels at lower costs. This *tournament theory* may explain the high levels of observed compensation at the top of hierarchies as well as the gap between the salaries of top executives and those of their immediate subordinates — the sub- ordinates accept less than their marginal product in order to remain in the race for the prize of a top executive's salary. Even Crystal, who does not accept this theory as empirically plausible, concedes:

> There is some intuitive support for the Tournament Theory. For example, think about how law firms run — or at least, how they use to run. A graduate fresh out of law school agreed to work for a law firm for close to slave wages in order to compete in a tournament that might end in a coveted partnership some seven years later. These young graduates might be argued to have contributed some of their true worth to a pool to be used to reward the winners of the tournament, the partners of the firm.[7] (1991b, 255.)

This lottery effect may be increasing in importance in firms as they reduce their layers of organization, thus increasing the numbers vying for promotion at each level. As Milgrom and Roberts put it:

> Firms' removal of layers of management has reduced the frequency with which promotions can be gained and the number of promotions that can be won....The leveling of organizational hierarchies has also probably increased the number of people at the lower rounds and, correspondingly, decreased the chances of winning promotion at these rounds. Both of these effects might well have adversely affected the incentives for middle-level managers. Any such negative incentive effects may have been offset by the impact of the recent increases in CEO compensation, however. Higher pay at the top of the hierarchy has increased the prize attached to winning in the last rounds and becoming an extremely well-paid senior executive, and thus may have increased middle-level managers' incentives to keep competing for promotions. (1992, 428.)

---

7 For an examination of the tournaments in US law firms, see Galanter and Palay (1991).

Thus, even if it could be shown for certain that executives were earning more than their marginal product, there is reason to suppose that this overpayment may be efficient. An inflated CEO compensation package may provide efficiencies by creating incentives elsewhere in the organization.

The Empirical Evidence

Although some analysts have recently examined executive pay in Canada,[8] most empirical studies of it are from the United States, where corporations have been compelled to disclose pay information since the early 1930s.[9] Indeed, the major US business periodicals (particularly *Fortune*, *Business Week*, and *Forbes*) publish spring cover stories largely devoted to listing the country's best-paid executives each year. These stories undoubtedly provoke strong reactions in their readers simply because of the remarkably high level of compensation that top executives earn. As already noted, Michael Eisner of Disney took home $203 million in 1993, which made him the highest-paid chief executive in the United States that year. His counterparts fared well also. The twenty-fifth-best-paid CEO in the United States that year, John Bryan of Sara Lee, had averaged more than $6 million annually in pay over the previous five years (Hardy 1994, 141). The Canadian evidence is less rich because disclosure of executive pay has been required for only a relatively short time. (Mandatory disclosure of the pay of each of the top five executives in publicly traded firms became law in Ontario only in 1993 — see the discussion below). As mentioned above, however, there are some notable data. Peter Munk, for example, has earned more than $30 million in a year, and Frank Stronach more than $40 million.

Although these figures are staggering, they are of dubious utility in assessing the appropriateness of executive compensation.

---

8 For example, KPMG (1995); Elitzur and Halpern (1995); and Magnan, St-Onge, and Thorne (1995).

9 Mandatory disclosure began with the *Securities Exchange Act of 1934*.

Very high salaries alone do not settle the issue or even significantly illuminate the matter. Consider, for example, that an *ex post* inquiry into Eisner's earnings at Disney would conclude that he earned monumental sums at the head of a thriving company. *Ex ante,* however, the compensation package he assumed was less striking, given that it was based on the performance of a company that, at the time, was a sluggish performer. While *ex post* Eisner earned astronomical amounts, this was the result of significant growth in the company (and shareholder wealth); it is difficult for an analyst to conclude that such a sum is excessive.

Brownstein and Panner (1992, 32) provide an interesting observation that further illustrates the weakness of rash inferences. When Time Warner CEO Steven Ross — to whom Crystal (1991b) dedicates a chapter entitled "The Prince of Pay" — was rumored to be seriously ill in December 1991, the firm's share price fell 4.75 points in five days (a drop of 1.0 point represented a loss of more than $90 million). In the same vein, Johnson et al. (1985) show that the stock market reaction to the unexpected death of a CEO is usually negative, indicating that he was not overpaid in the estimation of investors. Such evidence suggests a need for caution in casually asserting that executive compensation levels are too high.

A further reason for discounting the importance of "ten best-paid executive" lists is that they provide precisely what they say: extreme examples. Many executives are granted stock options which, when cashed, provide them with a significant, one-off gain; these sums are reported as their earnings that year, even though the options may have been granted over many years. As Milgrom and Roberts state:

> [T]he reported long-term incentive component of pay tends to be highly variable because the entire amount is reported in the year in which the gains are realized, even though they may be the result of several years' performance....Because the news stories tend to focus on the highest-paid executives in any year, this method of recording long-term compensation tends to bias the apparent income levels upward relative to the corresponding steady flows. (1992, 424–425.)

Thus, reports on the levels of compensation, although tantalizing, are not very helpful in assessing the efficacy of executive pay. Better evidence may come from other statistics, including those revealing the relationship between executive compensation and various measures of firm performance, the growth in executive compensation *vis-à-vis* corporate earnings or the pay of other workers, and international comparisons.

Executive Pay and Performance

Several studies examine the impact of corporate performance on the pay of senior executives. Given the significance of compensation schemes in aligning the interests of shareholders and managers, many commentators assert that, if compensation is not strongly linked to firm performance — in Loomis' language, if managers who "flop" are still rewarded "handsomely" — then compensation packages are inappropriate.

Several studies reach different conclusions on this matter. Milgrom and Roberts (ibid., 435n) note that the *Forbes* survey of 1990 found that the 25 highest-paid CEOs in the United States earned $2.26 for every $1,000 in revenues their companies generated, and $30.20 for every $1,000 in profits. Leonard examines pay patterns for more than 20,000 executives at 439 corporations between 1981 and 1985 and finds modest links between performance and executive pay; if a corporation's profits fell by $157 million (one standard deviation below the mean change in the sample), executive pay could be expected to fall by about 2 percent. He concludes:

> The level of executive pay cannot be justified in terms of contingent pay schemes when such a small proportion of executive pay is so weakly contingent. (1990, 21-S.)

Crystal takes a stronger view:

> [T]he bloated pay packages of American CEOs, with very few exceptions, contain hardly any pay risk. Those CEOs get paid hugely in good years and, if not hugely, then merely wonder-

> fully in bad years....Is the system rotten around the core or to the core? I'll take choice B. (1991b, 31.)

In general, Milgrom and Roberts report (1992, 438), when performance is based on accounting rates of return, the evidence across various studies is that top executives' pay typically increases by about 1 to 1¼ percent for every 1 percent increase in profit.

Jensen and Murphy (1990a) also find that executive pay is only weakly correlated with performance, but their conclusions are less adverse to the interests of executives. They study, among other data, the salaries and bonuses of 2,505 CEOs in 1,400 publicly held companies in the United States between 1974 and 1988, focusing on the change in executive pay associated with a change in shareholder wealth as measured by dividend payouts plus the change in the market value of the stock. They find that the median CEO's wealth (including changes in the probability of dismissal) increased by only $2.59 for every $1,000 increase in the wealth of shareholders. The figure fell to $1.93 when the executive's personal shareholdings were ignored. Using this focus on wealth, not profit, the authors find a correlation between performance and pay that is much weaker than previous studies had estimated,[10] which, they conclude, is evidence that CEOs' compensation levels are likely too low, probably for political reasons:

> How often do shareholder activists or union leaders denounce a corporate board for *under*paying the CEO? Not very often — and that's precisely the problem. Most critics of executive pay want it both ways. They want companies to link pay to performance, yet they also want to limit compensation to arbitrary amounts or some fuzzy sense of "what's fair." That won't work. Imposing a ceiling on salaries for outstanding performers inevitably means creating a floor for poor performers. Over time, by cutting off the upper and lower tails of the distribution, the entire pay-for-performance relation erodes. (1990a, 144.)

10 If the value of a company's stock is, for example, $1 billion, an increase in the present value of future profit of $1 million increases the value of the company by only 0.1 percent.

Elitzur and Halpern (1995) provide a study of the relationship between executive pay[11] and performance for 180 Canadian companies (in 13 industries) listed on the TSE. Like Jensen and Murphy, they find no strong link between compensation and performance. Indeed, they find no statistically significant relationship between the level of executive pay and firm performance in the sample companies. What they do find, however, is a positive correlation between the *change* in an executive's pay and performance from one period to the next.

Firm Size

The correlation between pay and firm size, a statistic perhaps related to the correlation between pay and performance, also inspires analysts to agreement about the numbers but disagreement about their implications. Almost always, the larger the size of the firm, the higher the level of executive compensation. As Milgrom and Roberts report:

> In study after study the same result appears, and the magnitude of the effect is remarkably stable across firms, industries, countries, and time periods: A 10 percent increase in sales results in about a 2 to 3 percent increase in salary plus bonus. Larger firms pay more, and when a firm grows, its pay rises to the level corresponding to its new size. (1992, 438, citing Rosen 1990.)

These uncontroversial figures, the authors continue, have generated diametrically opposed reactions. Some analysts claim that increased pay for increased firm size provides executives with perverse incentives; rather than maximize profits, they will maximize the size of the firm in order to feather their own nests with inevitably higher salaries. Other analysts suggest, however, that, if executives have a greater impact on larger corporations, given the greater number of

11 "Pay" in this study includes cash compensation (salary and bonus) but, because of data problems, excludes deferred compensation and long-term incentive plans.

people and processes affected by their decisions, then their marginal products are higher than those of executives at smaller corporations. Consequently, the larger the corporation, the higher the pay should be.

Growth in Executive Compensation

Growth in levels of executive compensation *vis-à-vis* growth in corporate earnings or in lower-level pay is frequently referred to as evidence either of the inappropriate extremes that compensation levels have reached or of the soundness of executive compensation.

During the 1980s, executive compensation in the United States certainly grew at remarkable rates. According to *Business Week* (Byrne 1991, 90), the average pay of the top two executives at 365 of the largest publicly held US corporations grew by 212 percent over the decade. During the same period, the average teacher saw his pay increase by only 95 percent, the average engineer by 73 percent, and the average factory worker by only 53 percent. Also in startling contrast, the earnings per share of the Standard and Poor's 500 companies rose only 78 percent. Over the 1989/90 year, the profits of the firms surveyed by *Business Week* fell 7 percent, while average executive pay rose by 3.5 percent. There is at least some evidence that these trends are present in Canada as well. A study of 239 companies listed on the TSE (KPMG 1995) finds that the total pay of CEOs increased by 18 percent in 1994, while Statistics Canada reports that the average pay of unionized workers rose by only 1.8 percent in the same year (Hameon 1995).

The disparity in growth rates between executives' and other workers' pay and between executives' pay and earnings per share is difficult to explain. As Byrne says, "[e]conomists who study the issue are at a loss to explain the growing disparities in rational terms" (1991, 90). If the productivity of the firm is growing generally, one would expect executives' pay, other employees' pay, and earnings per share to move in approximately the same direction. If all three statistics were at approximately appropriate levels at the beginning of the 1980s, the only rational economic explanation for the current disparity is that the productivity of executives has enjoyed idiosyncratic growth. On the other hand, if executive compensation was lower than appropriate at the beginning of the 1980s, then its rapid growth may simply be the result of the market's rational adjustment to a long-run equilibrium. Jensen and Murphy take the latter position, stating:

> Despite the headlines, top executives are not receiving record salaries and bonuses. Salaries and bonuses have increased over the last 15 years, but CEO pay levels are just now catching up to where they were 50 years ago. During the period 1934 through 1938, for example, the average salary and bonus for CEOs of leading companies on the New York Stock Exchange was $882,000 (in 1988 dollars). For the period 1982 through 1988, the average salary and bonus for CEOs of comparable companies was $843,000. (1990, 138–139.)

In brief, despite widespread agreement that executive compensation has indeed risen over recent years at a rate greater than other employee compensation or corporate earnings, there is disagreement over the reasons for this disparity.

Other Employees' Compensation

A related gauge of the heights that compensation levels have reached is the ratio of executives' pay to workers' pay. Crystal (1991b, 29) reports that, in 1991, the average executive's compensation was 130 times the average worker's — after he removed some peculiarly high executive compensation packages from his calculation.[12] Bok (1993, 102) notes that executive compensation was more than 100 times greater than the average wage in the United States in 1990.

Bok, Crystal, and others suggest that these ratios are exorbitant. Crystal (1991b, 24) points out that Plato once told Aristotle that "no one in a community should earn more than five times the pay of the

12 Including these outliers raised the ratio to 160 times the compensation of the average worker.

lowest-paid worker"; Crystal also notes that, a little more recently, Peter Drucker, a management theorist from California, suggested that no executive should earn more than 20 times the pay of her lowest-paid worker. These suggested ratios have been dwarfed by the pay earned by CEOs at many corporations. For example, in 1989, Steven Ross of Time Warner earned 9,000 times the pay of the average worker (ibid., 28); in 1990, Michael Eisner, who made $11.2 million that year, earned more in a day than the average Disney worker earned in a year (Byrne 1991, 91). Although these figures illustrate the significance of large sums of money, alone they fail to offer a normative benchmark with which to judge ratios, other than an elusive tweak of many people's sense of social justice. Like the growth in executive compensation levels, the growth in the ratios of executive compensation to average compensation provides a more enlightening picture. Crystal (1991b, 27) reports that, in 1974, an average CEO earned 35 times the pay of an average manufacturing worker, whereas in 1991 the multiple was nearly 120. The suggestion again is that, unless CEOs' productivity has enjoyed idiosyncratic growth, their compensation is at least suspect. Recall, however, Jensen and Murphy's contention that this growth in executive pay represents the market's finding its long-run equilibrium, after past undercompensation.

International Comparisons

Commentators repelled by the compensation levels of top executives, particularly in the United States, frequently cite the contrast between domestic and foreign executives' pay. Such comparisons were particularly encouraged in January 1992 when US President George Bush traveled to Japan accompanied by several of his country's top CEOs. As Bok states:

> The subject of executive compensation boiled over and became a public issue only after automobile executives traveled to Tokyo on a trade mission with President Bush. The sight of Lee Iacocca complaining [about unfair trade conditions] to leading Japanese

> executives making only a fraction of his pay was a spectacle that no reporter could resist. The stories that ensued provoked an angry reaction. (1995, 95.)

On its face, this reaction appears justified. Crystal (1991b, 28–29) states that, while executives in the United States are compensated at a rate equivalent to 130 times the pay of the average worker, the comparable figure in Japan is less than 20 and in the United Kingdom, less than 35.[13] Illustrating the point in a different way, the author continues, the average CEO of some of the largest 200 companies in the United States earned $2.4 million in 1991, which was seven times greater than the pay of the CEO of a large Japanese firm in that year. US executives are also paid better than their Canadian counterparts. According to Milgrom and Roberts (1992, 426), the average Canadian CEO earns approximately 65 percent of what a US CEO takes home.

These examples of executive pay in highly competitive countries are frequently viewed as particularly damning to defenders of managerial pay levels in the United States. The statistics also reveal that, although Canadian CEOs earn only a fraction of what US executives earn, they make more than their Japanese counterparts. These differences lead to conclusions such as Crystal's:

> Granted the cultures [of Japan and the United States are very different, and, unhappily, so are the products. The Japanese make better cars than we do, and they offer them at better prices. The Japanese culture may be different, but that different culture is killing us. So, to dismiss different executive pay levels in other countries against whom we compete every day in the international and domestic markets is plain fatuous. (1991b, 30.)

On the other hand, some commentators suggest that the contrast in pay between countries may be less dramatic than the statistics suggest. They assert that nonmonetary forms of compensation, such

---

13 According to Crystal, of the United Kingdom, Japan, Germany, and France, only the United Kingdom "show[s] signs of catching the US executive compensation virus, and it has only a mild case" (1991b, 28).

as club memberships and company housing, as well as much greater job security, explain much of the gap in pay between, for example, the United States and Japan. Liebtag states:

> In spite of a lower salary, however, the Japanese executive — still most often a male — is probably as well treated as his Western counterpart. He often receives many valuable perquisites, including a liberal expense account that covers some household expenses normally treated as personal obligations in the United States. In addition, the average executive continues to work or at least continues to draw a salary and receive perks many years longer than in the West....Finally, executives and managers are likely to be among the 35 percent of the Japanese work force that enjoys lifetime employment. (1991, 30.)

Thus, the compensation gap that critics cite as evidence of the egregious levels of executive pay in the West may be narrower than is often suggested — or indeed may not exist at all.

Tournament Evidence

Even if it could be conclusively proven that executive compensation exceeds reasonable economic benchmarks, such as marginal product, CEO sympathizers might respond by citing the tournament theory, which, as already discussed, holds that overpaying top executives creates efficient incentives throughout the organization, lowering the overall wage bill. The evidence on the tournament theory is mixed. To assess the effect of prize structures on incentives more generally, Ehrenberg and Bognanno examine the effect of prizes on the performance of professional golfers on the US Men's Professional Golf Association (PGA) Tour in 1984. They find evidence consistent with the tournament theory of compensation:

> Higher prize levels do lead, other things equal, to lower scores.... Given a player's performance in the first three rounds of the tournament, his performance in the last round also appears, other things equal, to depend on the marginal returns to effort he faces, with players who face larger marginal returns scoring

> lower. The level of prize money in tournaments also influences who enters the tournaments, with higher prize money attracting better...players. (1990a, 1322.)

These results should not be construed as peculiar to North American culture; Ehrenberg and Bognanno get very similar results from a study of the effects of prize structures on performance in the European PGA Tour (1990b).

Leonard finds evidence supporting the tournament theory of compensation in his study of the pay structures facing over 20,000 executives in 439 corporations between 1981 and 1985. The central proposition of the tournament theory is that mid-level executives are willing to accept lower wages in order to compete for future prizes. This seems likely to be true only if the prize increases as the probability of success falls; remote possibilities should have larger payoffs if they are to provide incentives. Leonard finds that as the promotion rate to the next level of the corporate hierarchy increases, the pay differential falls. He concludes:

> There is some evidence consistent with a tournament or lottery view of executive compensation. In such models, high pay in top executive positions is used to motivate lower-level executives to compete for promotions. The expected value to executives of such a scheme can be maintained if the pay differential across levels narrows while promotion probabilities increase.... Steeper pay differentials are indeed associated with lower promotion rates. (1990, 27–S.)

Crystal reaches the opposite conclusion, claiming that high pay for a CEO is typically accompanied by high pay throughout the firm. He says of the tournament theory:

> Nice theory, but it doesn't work....[R]esearch I have conducted shows that if the CEO is being paid above the market, so will his number two executive be paid above the market (although not perhaps by as much). And so will his number three executive. And on and on. (1991b, 256.)

In brief, despite some empirical support for the tournament theory, it is at least qualified by inconsistent evidence.

Other Evidence

Critics of executive compensation packages often focus their attention on the increased use of incentives, such as stock options, that are not accompanied by an according reduction in the base salary. Even Milgrom and Roberts, who are generally agnostic on the subject, note that,

> [b]ecause it often seems that large US firms add various long-term incentive pay components to their CEOs' compensation packages without obviously decreasing any of the other elements, knowledgeable observers of executive compensation consider these long-term programs the source of the relative jump in CEO pay in the 1980s. (1992, 427.)

They also observe an

> apparent tendency of boards to add new items to CEOs' compensation packages without adjusting the size of existing ones. Given this, a recommendation to increase the linkage between CEO and shareholder wealth through stock awards amounts to an invitation to bestow large amounts of stock on the CEOs, giving away even more of the shareholders' money to already well-paid executives. (Ibid., 441.)

The implication of these empirical observations is that executive compensation packages may be excessive.

Countering this assertion, however, is evidence of the efficacy of incentive programs. Market-based (rather than accounting-based) studies of these programs' effects recommend them. Tehranian and Waegelein (1985, 131) find that, after a company announces the introduction of executive compensation packages tying pay to accounting performance, the share price immediately jumps 11 percent. Brickley, Bhagat, and Lease (1985, 151) observe that adopting a long-term incentive plan increases the return to shareholders by 2 percent.

Abowd (1990, 52-S) finds from his study of more than 16,000 managers at 250 large corporations over the 1981–86 period that accounting performance is only weakly improved by an increase in the sensitivity of managerial pay to performance, but market responses (shareholder returns) are significant and positive. Although these studies do not rebut the assertion that compensation packages are excessive,[14] they do put in question the claim that such schemes are implemented *only* to feather executive nests.

The Law of Executive Compensation

Executive compensation is given within a country's framework of corporate law and its application. The legal situation in Canada,[15] as in the United States, sometimes has interesting effects.

Directors' Duties

The legal responsibility for setting the compensation of a corporation's executives rests with its board of directors. For example, the *Ontario Business Corporations Act (OBCA)* states:

> Subject to the articles, the by-laws or any unanimous shareholder agreement, the directors of a corporation may fix the remuneration of the directors, officers and employees of the corporation. (Sec. 137.)

Although this approach leaves wide scope for discretion, it is constrained by the fiduciary duty owed by directors and officers of the corporation. Under the *OBCA*, for example, all directors and officers must act "honestly and in good faith with a view to the best interests

14 They may be better than previous compensation schemes, but still excessive.

15 Canadian securities law falls largely under the jurisdiction of the provinces. The framework described here is Ontario's because almost all large public corporations in Canada are listed on the TSE.

of the corporation" (sec. 134). Thus, the legal obligation on directors is to set compensation levels for officers (and directors) that maximize the value of the company.

Although the obligation is clear, the enforceability of such a duty is suspect. Indeed, the law is not encouraging to those who wish to challenge the directors for breaching their fiduciary duty in setting compensation. In an important 1933 case (*Rogers v. Hill*) on the duties of directors with respect to compensation, the US Supreme Court held that a compensation scheme that had been ratified by shareholders 20 years earlier and that in 1930 had resulted in a payment of more than $1 million to the CEO of American Tobacco Company was "valid when adopted," although it also noted that freedom of contract "cannot...be used to justify payments of sums as salaries so large as in substance and effect to amount to spoliation or waste of corporate property." The case was later settled before it could be determined whether the scheme in question amounted to corporate waste, but the decision set a high standard for those wishing to challenge compensation schemes: if the scheme is originally valid, it will stand unless egregious.

The court's recognition of both "its power to limit executive pay, and its...reluctance to do so" (Shorten 1992, 149) has generally characterized judicial attitudes to the review of executive compensation. A later law suit over compensation to American Tobacco executives led the New York Supreme Court to write the following frequently cited passage on the limits of the courts' competence to review executive compensation packages:

> Assuming, *arguendo*, that the compensation should be revised, what yardstick is to be employed? Who or what is to supply the measuring rod? The conscience of equity?....Can equity be so arrogant as to hold that it knows more about managing this corporation than its shareholders?
>
> Yes, the court possesses the power to prune these payments, but openness forces the confession that the pruning would be synthetic and artificial rather than analytical or scientific. Whether or not it would be fair and just is highly dubious. No blueprints are furnished. The elements to be weighed are incalculable, the

> imponderables manifold. To act out of whimsy or caprice or arbitrariness would be more than inexact—it would be the precise antithesis of justice; it would be a farce. (*Heller v. Boylan*, 1941.)

Thus, while courts have long recognized their power to review compensation, they have also refrained from doing so, typically out of a mistrust of their own ability to handle such an issue.

Shareholders and Executive Compensation

Canadian corporate law permits shareholders direct participation in some corporate decisions through shareholder proposals and votes (see, for example, *OBCA*, sec. 99.) These votes may not, however, cover issues that are considered "ordinary business." Unfortunately for potentially activist shareholders, the setting of executive compensation is considered "ordinary business" in Canada, so direct shareholder participation through proposals is proscribed.

On the other hand, recent developments in securities law have enhanced the ability of shareholders to monitor directors' decisions about executive compensation. In October 1993, the Ontario government adopted an order-in-council making various reforms to the *Securities Act* regulations. A fundamental change was the requirement that the compensation of the CEO and the four highest-paid executive officers of Ontario issuers be disclosed in a variety of tables, rather than in a potentially confusing narrative.[16] The issuer is also required to disclose details of the repricing of any options or SARs in the past year and any other repricings over the past ten years and to give reasons for these decisions. To aid the assessment of the propriety of the composition of the compensation committee, which the board frequently appoints to handle its compensation decisions, the issuer is compelled to outline conflicts such as *interlocks* (for

16 The tables required by the new rules include a summary compensation table, a long-term incentive plan awards table, an options/SARs granted table, an options/SARs exercised table, a table for defined benefit and actuarial plans, and a table for executive indebtedness.

example, two directors sit on at least two compensation committees together) present in the committee. Finally, the issuer must provide graphs plotting the shareholders' return alongside the returns to a comparable market or industry index. Aside from these technical requirements, the issuer is also required to outline the compensation philosophy of the corporation, including a discussion of pay/performance linkages.

These reforms bring Ontario law in line with the revisions adopted by the US Securities and Exchange Commission (SEC) in October 1992.[17]

Reform Proposals

The legal framework just outlined has been criticized in many quarters. Critics take aim particularly at the potential for conflicts of interest on the board. Other commentators focus their suggested reforms on shareholders, the courts, and tax law.

Boards and Executive Compensation

That the potential for unhealthy conflicts of interest over compensation decisions exists on many boards is undebatable. One cause is the presence of insiders. Officers of the corporation frequently sit on the board. This situation creates a clear conflict of interest if all directors vote on compensation — the inside directors then vote on their own compensation. Despite this opportunity for blatant self-dealing, the law does not distinguish between inside and outside directors; rather, it states that the board as a whole is responsible for compensation decisions (see, for example, *OBCA*, sec. 137).

In recognition of this potential conflict, many firms establish compensation committees comprised solely of outside directors to make recommendations about compensation to the board as a whole.

17 For an extensive outline of these US reforms, see Bakris (1993).

Insider problems still exist, however. Milgrom and Roberts explain one that is obvious: "Often, but not always, the compensation committee is composed exclusively of outside directors....Nevertheless, the CEO is usually a member of the committee *ex officio*" (1992, 434). Indeed, the CEO frequently makes the initial compensation suggestions for the committee to deliberate.

Other self-dealing problems are more subtle. In many corporations, for example, the chairman of the board is also the company's CEO. Thus, the composition of the board is largely controlled by the company's executives, a situation that implies the possibility of stacking the board with directors friendly to the CEO.

A phenomenon frequently observed, particularly in a relatively small economy such as Canada's, is interlocking directorships, whereby directors may be "top executives of other corporations on whose boards the chief executive officers may sit" (Elson 1993, 942). Such a situation is clearly tainted by the possibility of an "I'll scratch your back if you scratch mine" mentality toward executive compensation, which may influence the CEO to search out such directors.[18]

Even if the directors are not predisposed to the executives through social connections or interlocks, directorships have advantages with which individuals may be reluctant to part. Some are nonpecuniary. The prestige associated with the role alone may leave directors reluctant to endanger their positions on boards, and conflicts with executives over such a potentially volatile matter as executive pay may be one way to endanger these positions, particularly if the CEO is chairman of the board.

Of rising concern are the increasingly attractive pecuniary advantages of directorships. *Business Week* reports that, in 1990, the average pay of directors of 352 companies was $32,252 for only 92 hours of work (Dobrzynski 1991, 94), while the directors of Pepsico, for example, each took home $78,000 that year. This money is

18 The conflicts inherent in these insider situations led the general counsel to the California Public Employees' Retirement System to observe that having a CEO as chairman of the board is "like grading your own papers" (quoted in McMenamin 1994, 143).

not insignificant to many people. For example, the dean of Northwestern University's Kellogg School of Management earned at least a third more from his service on several boards than he did from the university (Lublin 1991, B-1). In Canada, too, directorships have the potential to be very lucrative. For accepting directorships at American Barrick and Horsham, two companies controlled by Peter Munk, Brian Mulroney was granted stock options that, if exercised when granted, were worth $1.5 million;[19] this came on top of his pay of $12,000 per year per directorship, $600 per meeting attended at American Barrick, and $1,000 per meeting attended at Horsham (McKenna 1993, A1).

With such sums being paid out, recent years have seen an increased focus on director compensation. As McKenna reports, Mulroney's compensation "raised concerns among compensation specialists and shareholders-rights activists" (ibid.). One concern is about sheer excess and the suboptimal use of corporate resources in director compensation, just as in executive compensation. Another concern is that these pay packages may actually induce suboptimal behavior simply by their level. The risk of possible ousting from the board and subsequent loss of such significant pecuniary advantages may leave otherwise independent directors reluctant to challenge executives' suggestions, particularly those about executive compensation. Although the board is responsible for setting directors' pay, in practice that pay is approved by the board but suggested by the CEO. Well-paid directors may show their gratitude for the CEO's largesse by approving correspondingly high executive pay. Thus, the recent tendency toward increased pay for directors may both waste corporate assets in itself and provide them with undesirable incentives that lead to further waste of those assets.

Another problem with the potential influence of executives rests with the increasingly frequent use of compensation consultants, who are often hired by the CEO to assist compensation committees.

19 None of these options could be exercised for a year; after that, a third of the Horsham options and a quarter of the American Barrick options could be exercised annually.

The danger is that the consultant and, therefore, the compensation committee will be influenced by executives of the company. Consider the following anecdote Crystal tells about his own experience as a practicing compensation consultant:

> I recommended that [the CEO] cut his salary to $100,000 [from $160,00] to make room for a normal 60%-of-salary bonus opportunity. I explained to him he would in a year of normal performance earn what he was earning now; in a year of above-normal performance, he would earn more than he was earning now; and, fair is fair, in a year of below-normal performance, he would earn less than he was earning now.
>
> The CEO did not take kindly to my suggestion. First, he tried to argue me out of the recommendation....But he wasn't successful. So he looked me in the eye and posed a question to me that I will never forget: "Just who do you think is paying your bills, anyway?"....[W]e broke up, and I have never heard from him again. I'd bet, however, that he found another compensation consultant who was willing to recommend that the company adopt a new annual incentive plan without requiring executives to cut back on their base salaries. (1991b, 219.)

Aside from such explicit conflicts of interest, some commentators contend that most directors are relatively uninformed about the intricacies of executive compensation,[20] and have no significant incentives to learn about them. Unlike the astronomical salaries that occur in, for example, professional sports, the pay of executives results not from a negotiation between two parties who have a financial interest in the outcome (such as the team owner and a professional baseball player),[21] but rather between the executive who has a direct financial interest in the outcome and directors who have little at stake financially other than the potential of being ousted from the board.

20 As Barris states, "Because these committees are composed of other executives, not compensation specialists, they often lack technical expertise in compensation issues" (1992, 76).

21 See the discussion in Crystal (1991b, 31–37).

One result of this asymmetry is that directors, rather than negotiating earnestly on behalf of shareholders, are content to rely on comparison studies. They may even ask the compensation consultant to set pay higher than the average "to attract a better grade of executive." That suggestion often originates with the incumbent executives, according to Crystal, who comments:

> It wouldn't be so bad if some companies, as a matter of policy, paid above the average so long as other companies, also as a matter of policy, paid below the average. But that almost never happens. In one survey I conducted some years back of one hundred companies' pay policies, thirty-five stated that they were aiming for the 75th percentile of the distribution, sixty-five state that they were aiming for the competitive average, and none stated that they were aiming for a position below the average. (Ibid., 223.)

In such a situation, executive pay will race to the top as lesser-paid executives receive raises to the median level or above, increasing next year's median pay, which, in turn, increases the raises for executives the following year.

In sum, the setting of executive pay is rife with potential conflicts of interest and inherently flawed because of the divergence in economic interests between the executives, who are directly concerned with compensation, and directors, whose interest is attenuated.

Suggestions for Reforming Boards

A viable solution to the potential problems raised by the legal framework for executive compensation is easy to state but more difficult to implement. As Elson puts it:

> The solution lies in loosening the outside directors' ties to management and recreating a vital and independent board, which will result in active oversight, not passive agreement. A way must be found to reinvigorate the outside director who traditionally acted in the shareholders' interests by directing management. (1993, 942.)

The challenge is to suggest reforms that would accomplish this uncontroversial solution.

Directors' Fees. Elson, who believes that the way directors are paid contributes significantly to the problem, suggests that paying them in equity, not cash, would better align their interests with those of the shareholders whom they represent. Furthermore, to enhance their independence by diminishing the threat of removal from the board, he suggests that their terms be extended. He states:

> [C]orporations should pay their directors their annual fees in restricted company stock. In a few years, each outside director will have accumulated a reasonably substantial portfolio and, therefore, will possess a powerful financial incentive to act more independently of management. Additionally, directors' term lengths must be significantly extended to ensure that their equity positions (or potential positions) will reach the levels necessary to influence their decision-making and to mitigate the chilling effect of a management threat not to renominate that frequent elections create. (Ibid., 944.)

Compensation Committees. Other commentators focus on increasing the independence of compensation committees. Currently, most such committees operate by reacting to proposals put before them, either by the executives themselves or by consultants hired by the executives. As Barris says, "committees themselves rarely initiate the plans"(1992, 76). Crystal proposes a more proactive approach: that compensation committees be "mandated" to hire their own compensation consultants who "would not be permitted ties of any sort with the company's management" (1991, 242–243). To encourage monitoring of particular consultants, a company would have to include in its proxy statement each year the name of its consultant and if he were fired, the company's reasons for doing so, and the consultant's reply. Such reforms, Crystal suggests, would reduce the direct and indirect (through "captured" consultants) influence that executives often have over the compensation committee.

Like Elson, Crystal takes aim at director compensation, although his concern is with how much directors are paid. He suggests setting their pay with reference to external factors:

> To dampen the incestuous relationship between the pay of the CEO and the pay of the outside directors, boards should adopt policies that peg their own pay to the median of a group of like companies....In short, they should insulate themselves from being bribed by a CEO who is bent on improving his own pay package. (Ibid., 245.)

US Representative Ed Markey proposes another reform aimed at controlling the capture of directors: that legislation restrict the members of compensation committees to outside directors;[22] furthermore, to control interlocking directorships, directors would be limited in the number of compensation committees they could serve on simultaneously (Jones 1993, 1B).

Other Proposals. Other proposed reforms are aimed more generally at providing directors with a legal framework that would better induce them to act in the best interests of the shareholders, not of management or of themselves. Although I lack space for a survey of these more general reforms here, one frequently advocated proposal deserves mention. Many commentators recommend that a CEO be prohibited from serving as chairman of the board or perhaps as a director at all.[23] This reform is addressed at minimizing the potential for the capture of other board members by an insider acting as their boss.

22 This was also recommended by the London Stock Exchange's Greenbury Committee in its report on executive pay. See "Fat Cats and Their Cream," *The Economist*, July 22, 1995, p. 19.

23 For a discussion of this proposition, see McMenamin (1994). Crystal (1991b, 245) discusses Jay Lorsch's suggestion that CEOs not be permitted to serve on boards at all.

Shareholders

Although most commentators agree that the concern about excessive executive compensation lies with the potential for conflicts on the board of directors, some choose to focus their reform efforts on other institutions that may be able to control the board's behavior. Increasingly, shareholders are being targeted as protectors of their own interests, and policies are being suggested to facilitate their activism.

The central drawback to relying on shareholders to fend for themselves is the familiar collective action problem: since each shareholder in a widely held corporation receives only a fraction of the benefits of controlling compensation excess, each has only a suboptimal incentive to undertake costly monitoring and disciplining activities. As Daniels puts it, "Since the benefits of governance activity are not confined to the activists, shareholders will be encouraged to remain rationally apathetic" (1994, 44). Reforms, therefore, frequently center on reducing the cost of monitoring and/or disciplining actions.

Increased Disclosure. One such reform that has been adopted in both Canada and the United States is increased disclosure of compensation packages. With the cost of investigating the propriety of executive compensation packages reduced through mandated disclosure (including an explanation of the firm's pay philosophy and comparisons with the performance of similarly situated firms), larger shareholders, particularly institutional ones, may face sufficient incentives to act to control executive compensation, notwithstanding collective action problems. As Daniels states:

> The revised regulations [on disclosure] will enhance the incentives of both directors and institutional shareholders to review and control executive compensation arrangements. Under the sunlight of heightened disclosure, compensation committees will be encouraged to devise compensation arrangements that meet shareholder expectations. (Ibid., 41.)

Optimism seems particularly justified in Canada, where institutional investors frequently hold a significant percentage of a company's shares.[24] Although each can still reap only a fraction of the benefits from activism, collectively they can realize a much higher fraction than institutional investors in the United States, who typically hold a smaller percentage of shares.[25] Nevertheless, US institutional shareholders do frequently challenge compensation agreements, and commentators often look to them to play such a role (see, for example, Barris 1992).

Increased Shareholder Voice. Although disclosure rules reduce the cost of monitoring executive compensation, they do not help in reducing the cost of activities designed to alter compensation packages. In the United States, the SEC has changed its policy of disallowing shareholder proposals regarding executive compensation (for discussion, see Ragsdale 1993, 551). Shareholders may now vote in their proxy materials on "advisory" (nonbinding) shareholder proposals regarding executive compensation. SEC Chairman Richard Breeden outlines the reasoning behind this policy shift:

> Hopefully, this decision will bring a market solution to a market problem by allowing the affected private sector groups — management, directors and shareholders — to resolve the compensation questions in each company on a case-by-case basis without government regulation. (Quoted in Barris 1992, 91.)

Proponents of combining increased disclosure with increased scope for shareholder voice hope that these reforms will reduce the cost to shareholders of controlling executive pay.

---

24 For discussions of the role of institutional investors in the Canadian setting, see Daniels and Waitzer (1994); and MacIntosh (1994).

25 Barris (1992, 89) reports that the top 20 institutional investors in the United States hold only about 16 percent of the shares in the ten largest US corporations

Drawbacks. Others argue, however, that such reforms are at best unnecessary and at worst liable to lead to what Pound calls "uncertainty and dislocation" (1992, A12). He cites the case of Westinghouse as an example of the potential for shareholder activism that existed under the US regime before the recent SEC reforms. Various institutional investors and other shareholder activists objected to the company's compensation structure and threatened significant unrest (such as a variety of shareholder proposals) unless the problem was addressed. In response, Westinghouse executives met with the concerned shareholders and subsequently altered the compensation arrangements with the aid of an independent compensation committee that used its own consultants. The incident illustrates, Pound contends, that the system was effective without reform.

Brownstein and Panner are sympathetic to this view. Of the SEC reforms, they state:

> While significant, this change in long-standing SEC policy is dwarfed by the already powerful voice of institutional investors. Even before the regulatory changes were made, companies met with their largest shareholders to discuss the way senior executives should be compensated. (1992, 34.)

Other commentators express concern about the costs of disclosure. Some cite the cost of compiling the tables and charts:

> [I]t is important to ask the question: disclosure at what cost? And, it appears that one thing is certain about the new [SEC] regulations — that is that companies will incur increased costs in compliance. (Ragsdale 1993, 569.)

Others point to the cost to the executives from an invasion of their privacy. The CEO of Stelco, for example, says that requiring disclosure "does tend to invade privacy" (quoted in Stinson 1993, B1). Some critics go so far as to worry that disclosure of high salaries will increase dangers of kidnapping (ibid.).[26] In brief, although many

26 Ken Hugesson, a Toronto compensation specialist, replies that criminals do not need a prospectus to find Forest Hill (a wealthy residential area of Toronto) (Rusk 1993, B1).

commentators applaud encouraging investor activism with increased disclosure, others would prefer a more cautious approach.

The Courts

As discussed above, the law requires that directors act in the best interest of the corporation. Granting excessive (not simply high) pay packages to executives is clearly not in the best interest of the corporation, and directors who act in such a fashion are in apparent contravention of the law. Yet, as also noted above, the courts have been historically reluctant to interfere with the business judgment of directors, so long as proper procedures have been followed. Many commentators advocate reform of this passive judicial approach.

In a relatively early paper on controlling compensation excess, Vagts (1983) suggests that the courts have the potential to play a significant role in overseeing boards of directors in setting executive pay. He and others (for example, Barris 1992; Bogus 1993; Shorten 1992) note that the courts, although not compensation experts, have shown readiness and ability to rule on excessive compensation in closely held corporations and in tax cases. These commentators suggest that, although judging whether compensation levels are excessive is not an easy task for the courts, it is possible and indeed undertaken in other contexts. The courts should, therefore, hold directors to a standard stricter than that to which they are currently held. Vagts suggests that, in cases in which the rules of corporate governance and shareholder activism are inadequate,

> [a]s a last resort we look to the courts....[C]ourts need to understand that while judgments on the excessiveness of executive compensation are not easy to make, they usually are not impossible....[C]ourts can and should carefully scrutinize compensation that is substantially out of line and prune off the abnormal amount when not justified by special risks run by the executive recipients or special contributions made by them. If the courts act, even occasionally, to trim compensation it will, in turn, be easier for compensation committees to tell executives that they simply cannot gratify their pocketbooks and egos as much as the executives demand. (1983, 275–276.)

Tax Law

Some commentators, despairing of reforming the governance of executive compensation either internally through board or shareholder solutions or externally through the courts, suggest the admittedly more blunt instrument of tax policy. Tax law, allege supporters of this approach, could make high salaries more expensive to the corporation; consequently, firms would use greater care in setting compensation.

In the United States, where executive compensation has attracted substantial political attention, as many as six compensation related bills were before Congress in 1992 (Barris 1992, 79). Eventually, Congress passed the *Omnibus Budget Reconciliation Act of 1993*, which eliminates corporate tax deductions for executive compensation greater than $1 million that is unrelated to performance. As Barris explains:

> The theory behind these bills is simple: Public policy does not support extreme distortions in income distribution, and taxpayers should not have to subsidize high-level executives through business tax deductions. (Ibid.)

Conclusion

This paper has reviewed some of the central theoretical, empirical, and legal literature on executive compensation.

The theoretical literature is both vast and complex. There is no simple economic optimum for a compensation package. In some situations, an emphasis on bonuses is appropriate to motivate executives to put forth optimum effort; in other cases, the private risk facing the risk-averse executive as a result of such an emphasis encourages suboptimal risk taking. Stock options can mitigate the risk associated with providing executives with incentives, but they may encourage managers to undertake investments that are excessively speculative. In yet other situations, paying executives more than their marginal product may minimize the overall wage bill by establishing a prize over which lower-level employees will compete.

Thus, the only firm conclusion to be drawn is that compensation is potentially very important to the health of a company, but no simple formula can capture the optimum arrangement in every situation. As *The Economist* states, "pay can have a powerful effect on managerial behaviour. It is worth getting right" ("Fat Cats and Their Cream," July 22, 1995, p. 19). This may, however, be easier said than done.

The empirical evidence is mixed. Although compensation levels, particularly in the United States, can be very high, this fact does not in itself indicate that they are excessive. Of more concern is the fairly consistent finding that performance and pay appear to be only weakly linked; if this is true, current compensation packages may be providing too few positive incentives. Also of note is the apparent divergence in the growth of the pay of executives and of other employees over recent years. Although some commentators view this divergence as evidence of executives' greed, other suggest that the market is correcting for their historical underpayment. International comparisons are inconclusive as well. Some analysts find that US executives (and, to a lesser extent, Canadian executives) are overpaid relative to their Japanese counterparts, but others claim that this divergence disappears if perks are included fully in pay. The tournament theory of executive pay also draws mixed reactions: some find evidence supporting it, others claim the theory does not work. There is, however, fairly strong market evidence that the introduction of incentive plans to executive pay increases expected profits as reflected in share values. This increase at least suggests that, although incentive pay may be unnecessarily high, it has positive effects on shareholder income.

The legal literature focuses on the potential for self-dealing present in the corporate law regime governing executive compensation. The suggestion is that executives have the potential to unduly influence directors, who have at best only an attenuated financial stake in the compensation decision. Reformers suggest that boards, and particularly their compensation committees, be redesigned to encourage independence from executives. They also recommend that the potential power of institutional investors be more fully realized by facilitating monitoring and other forms of activism. Some commentators urge the courts to reject passivity and actively review excessive compensation packages. Finally, others suggest changes to the tax laws designed to limit executive pay.

An appropriate conclusion to draw from this survey is that simplistic conclusions about executive compensation are unlikely to advance the debate; it is far too complex for black-and-white thinking.

Future Research

There are several potentially fruitful areas for future research on executive compensation. One relates to the theory of compensation and motivation. As discussed above, bonuses and other forms of contingent pay may induce optimal effort from an executive by offering an opportunity for personal gain. On the other hand, contingent pay may induce risk-averse managers to choose safe but sub-profit maximizing investments.

According to the latter theory, one would expect that particularly risky industries would not offer risky pay structures. In reality, however, no correlation between safer pay packages and risky industries is immediately apparent. Further research might identify this lack of correlation more clearly, leading to a possible alternative theory of contingent pay. If a job is inherently risky and the pay schedule cannot entirely insure against this risk (perhaps because of the managerial labor market), risk aversion may be an undesirable feature in a manager. To account for this, risky pay packages may be offered not to induce optimal effort but to deter risk-averse candidates. If the variance of executive pay is sufficiently large, risk-averse individuals may be deterred from pursuing such positions, while more risk-neutral candidates may find such a package attractive. In other words, risky pay may be associated with risky management positions not to induce effort but to screen out risk-averse managers.

Another potential area of future study is the effect of stock options. Some people say that such compensation is risk free for managers. This is not true. If the firm performs well, the options will be valuable; if it performs poorly, the options will have little value. Thus, what options limit is out-of-pocket risk; the manager who receives them still risks forgone gains if the company does not perform well. Yet, although a forgone gain is equivalent to an incurred loss in theoretical economics, behavioral studies suggest that an out-of-pocket loss is more significant to many people than an opportunity cost (see, for example, Knetsch 1989). A study of the risk properties of stock options might be informed by an analysis of this perceived difference between types of cost.

A further area of study with respect to stock options is their repricing when share prices fall. Some commentators conclude that such repricing is evidence of the influence that executives wield over the board. Consider, however, the incentive properties of an "underwater" option (one in which the strike price is greater than the share price). If the option price is much higher then the share price, an executive may face two choices. She may simply give up on ever exercising it, in which case the option has no incentive effect. Alternatively, she may decide to undertake overly risky investments — sub-profit-maximizing — because her options will only be valuable if the company enjoys a very large payoff. Given the undesirability of either of these incentives, repricing underwater options may be a rational adjustment. Yet this consideration raises a more fundamental issue. If an executive knows that it is rational for a firm to reprice underwater options, the incentive effect of the options may be attenuated; if the firm is successful, the manager will be paid off at the current option price, but if the firm is unsuccessful, the manager will eventually be paid off at an adjusted price. Commitment problems may thus exist for a firm that offers options as incentives to executives.

A different area of study might be the role of institutional investors. Although many people claim that such investors have suboptimal incentives to monitor compensation since each individual can reap only a fraction of the total gains from diligent monitoring, nevertheless such monitoring is observed. A possible explanation is reputation. For example, if the California Public Employees' Retirement System — which is known for strict monitoring and negotiating over executive compensation in the United States — owns only 2 or 3 percent of one company's shares, its interest in monitoring appears trivial. Yet if, by challenging compensation in one company, it gains a reputation for monitoring compensation diligently, other companies in which it owns stock may be reluctant to grant excessive compensation packages.

Commentators frequent assert that increased disclosure of executive pay will encourage increased shareholder activism and more appropriate compensation schemes. Some suggest, however, that disclosure may in fact contribute to higher pay. John McNeil, chairman and CEO of Sun Life, states that his "informed opinion" is that "executive compensation levels in countries where disclosure is not required generally are significantly lower than in countries where disclosure is required" (1993, A33). An interesting area of study would be to examine the evidence on whether this opinion is true or not, and if it is, why. The previously described theory of the race to the top suggests that since no boards aim for below-average compensation, average executive compensation will rise from year to year. Disclosure may encourage this phenomenon.

The valuation of executive compensation also needs more study. There may be technical problems in assessing *ex ante* the value of some of the pay packages, especially those including stock options. Given that the options granted to executives are typically illiquid, it is difficult to determine their market-clearing price. The mathematical model frequently relied on to value these options, the Black-Scholes model, is very complex and would likely be inaccessible to many executives and shareholders attempting to value options. Furthermore, it requires variables, such as the volatility of the price of the stock on which the option is based, that are themselves difficult to estimate. There may also be problems with the model itself; in markets where options are traded, the price often deviates significantly from the Black-Scholes estimate.

Another area for further study is the effect of tax laws on executive compensation. Although the economics of compensation suggests a variety of compensation tools to achieve a variety of objectives, tax laws may limit the choices. For example, if options are granted with the objective of inducing an executive eventually to purchase shares of the company and retain them, Canadian law may discourage this. When a Canadian taxpayer exercises an option, any gain potentially realized if the shares were sold is immediately imputed to taxable income, whether the shares are actually sold or not. Given that most people face some liquidity constraints, this law may encourage executives to sell the shares bought with options shortly after their exercise in order to realize the cash necessary to pay their taxes. Encouraging stock ownership through the granting of options may thus be discouraged.

Another issue arises with the tax treatment of supplemental executive retirement plans (SERPs), which are amounts paid to executives above the limit that the company can legally deduct as a pension expense for tax purposes. The promise of rich pensions may provide valuable incentives for an executive to remain loyal to a firm, yet the cap on pensions for tax purposes may obstruct such schemes. On the other hand, if self-dealing problems arise in the setting of SERPs, the fact that they are not deductible to the firm may exacerbate their harm to shareholders.

Although executive compensation has been the subject of considerable controversy, as this review has shown, the issues suggested here and others may present worthwhile topics for further study.

References

Abowd, J. 1990. "Does Performance-Based Managerial Compensation Affect Corporate Performance?" *Industrial and Labor Relations Review* 43 (February, special issue): 52-S–73-S.

Bakris, M. "Executive Compensation Disclosure: The SEC's Newest Weapon in Its Arsenal against Executive Compensation Abuses." *University of Detroit Mercy Law Review* 71(1): 105–153.

Barris, L. 1992. "The Overcompensation Problem: A Collective Approach to Controlling Executive Pay." *Indiana Law Journal* 68 (1): 59–100.

Berle, A., and G. Means. 1933. *The Modern Corporation and Private Property*. New York: MacMillan.

Bogus, C. 1993. "Excessive Executive Compensation and the Failure of Corporate Democracy." *Buffalo Law Review* 41 (1): 1–83.

Bok, D. 1993. *The Cost of Talent*. Toronto: The Free Press.

Brickley, J., S. Bhagat, and R. Lease. 1985. "The Impact of Long-Range Compensation Plans on Shareholder Wealth." *Journal of Accounting and Economics* 7 (1–3): 115–129.

Brownstein A., and M. Panner. 1992. "Who Should Set CEO Pay? The Press? Congress? Shareholders?" *Harvard Business Review*, May-June, pp. 28–38.

Burchman, S. 1991. "Choosing Appropriate Performance Measures." In F. Foulkes, ed., *Executive Compensation: A Strategic Guide for the 1990s.* Boston: Harvard Business School Press.

Burroughs, B., and J. Helyar 1990. *Barbarians at the Gate*. New York: HarperPerennial.

Buyniski, T. 1991. "The Past, Present, and Possible Future Role of Executive Stock Compensation." In F. Foulkes, ed., *Executive Compensation: A Strategic Guide for the 1990s.* Boston: Harvard Business School Press.

Byrne, J. 1991. "The Flap over Executive Pay." *Business Week*, May 6, pp. 90–96.

Crystal, G. 1991a. "CEO Compensation: The Case of Michael Eisner." In F. Foulkes, ed., *Executive Compensation: A Strategic Guide for the 1990s.* Boston: Harvard Business School Press.

———. 1991b. *In Search of Excess: The Overcompensation of American Executives*. New York: W.W. Norton.

Daniels, R. 1994. "Executive Compensation: Perhaps Company Managers Aren't Paid Enough...." *Canadian Investment Review*, spring, pp. 41–46.

Daniels R., and E. Waitzer. 1994. "Challenges to the Citadel: A Brief Overview of Recent Trends in Canadian Corporate Governance." *Canadian Business Law Journal* 23 (1): 23–44.

Dobrzynski, J. 1991. "Directors' Pay Is Becoming an Issue, Too." *Business Week*, May 6, p. 94.

Ehrenberg R., and M. Bognanno. 1990a. "Do Tournaments Have Incentive Effects?" *Journal of Political Economy* 98 (6): 1307–1324.

———. 1990b. "The Incentive Effects of Tournaments Revisited: Evidence from the European PGA Tour." *Industrial and Labor Relations Review* 43 (February, special issue): 74-S–88-S.

Elitzur R., and P. Halpern. 1995. "Executive Compensation and Firm Value." In R. Daniel, and R. Morck, eds., *Corporate Decision Making in Canada*. Calgary: University of Calgary Press.

Elson, C. 1993. "Executive Compensation — A Board-Based Solution." *Boston College Law Review* 34 (5): 437–496.

Fama, E. 1980. "Agency Problems and the Theory of the Firm." *Journal of Political Economy* 88 (2): 288–367.

———, and M. Jensen. 1983. "Separation of Ownership and Control." *Journal of Law and Economics* 26 (2): 301–325.

Galanter M., and T. Palay. 1991. *Tournament of Lawyers: The Transformation of the Big Law Firm*. Chicago: University of Chicago Press.

Gunderson, M. 1993. *Labour Market Economics: Theory, Evidence and Policy in Canada*. 3rd ed. Toronto: McGraw-Hill Ryerson.

Hameon, J. 1995. "Bosses get 18% raises." *Toronto Star*, September 7, p. B1.

Hardy, E. 1994 "Marathon Men." *Forbes*, May 23, pp. 140–142.

Holmstrom, B. 1979. "Moral Hazard and Observability." *Rand Journal of Economics* 10 (spring): 74–91.

Jensen, M., and W. Meckling. 1976. "Theory of the Firm: Managerial Behavior, Agency Costs and Ownership Structure." *Journal of Financial Economics* 3 (3): 305–360.

———, and K. Murphy. 1990a. "CEO Incentives — It's Not How Much You Pay, but How." *Harvard Business Review*, May-June, pp. 138–149.

———, and K. Murphy. 1990b. "Performance Pay and Top-Management Incentives." *Journal of Political Economy* 98 (2): 225–264.

Johnson, W., et al. 1985. "An Analysis of the Stock Price Reaction to Sudden Executive Deaths: Implications for the Managerial Labor Market." *Journal of Accounting and Economics* 7 (1): 151–174.

Jones, D. 1993. "Legislator takes on boardroom." *USA Today*, March 26, p. 1B.

Kay, I. 1992, *Value at the Top*. New York: Harper Business.

Knetsch, J. 1989. "The Endowment Effect and Evidence of Non-Reversible Indifference Curves." *American Economic Review* 79 (5): 1277–1284.

KPMG. 1995. *Executive Compensation Practices in the TSE 300 Companies 1995*. Toronto.

Lambert, R., and D. Larcker. 1991. "Executive Compensation, Corporate Decision Making, and Shareholder Wealth: A Review of the Evidence." In F. Foulkes, ed., *Executive Compensation: A Strategic Guide for the 1990s*. Boston: Harvard Business School Press.

Lazear, E., and S. Rosen. 1981. "Rank-Order Tournaments as Optimum Labor Contracts." *Journal of Political Economy* 89 (5): 841–864.

Leonard, J. 1990. "Executive Pay and Firm Performance." *Industrial and Labor Relations Review* 43 (February, special issue): 13-S–29-S.

Liebtag, W. 1991. "Compensating Executives: The Development of Responsible Management." In F. Foulkes, ed., *Executive Compensation: A Strategic Guide for the 1990s.* Boston: Harvard Business School Press.

Loomis, C. 1982. "The Madness of Executive Compensation." *Fortune*, July 12, pp. 42–46.

Lublin, J. 1991. "While outside directors' pay increases, independence from managers may fade." *Wall Street Journal*, April 22, p. B-1.

MacIntosh, J. 1994. "The Role of Institutional and Retail Shareholders in Canadian Capital Markets." *Osgoode Hall Law Journal* 32 (2): 371–472.

McKenna, B. 1993. "Mulroney stock options could provide bonanza." *Globe and Mail* (Toronto), January 13, p. A1.

Mackenzie, W. 1995. "Options, Too Much of a Good Thing?" *Corporate Governance Review* 7 (3): 15.

McMenamin, B. 1994. "Safety Valve." *Forbes*, May 23, p. 143.

McNeil, J. 1993. "Why make executives disclose their salaries?" *Globe and Mail* (Toronto), October 29, p. A33.

Magnan, M., S. St-Onge, and L. Thorne. 1995. "A Comparative Analysis of the Determinants of Executive Compensation between Canadian and US Firms." *Industrial Relations—Quebec* 50: 297–317.

Milgrom, P., and J. Roberts. 1992. *Economics, Organization and Management*. Englewood Cliffs, NJ: Prentice Hall.

Murphy, K. 1986. "Top Executives Are Worth Every Nickel They Get." *Harvard Business Review*, March-April, pp. 125–132.

Pound, J. 1992. "Westinghouse lights boardroom path." *Wall Street Journal*, December 11, p. A12.

Pritchard, T. 1994. "Magna chief takes the lead at pay window." *Globe and Mail* (Toronto), November 1, p. B1.

Ragsdale, M. 1993. "Executive Compensation: Will the New SEC Disclosure Rules Control 'Excessive' Pay at the Top?" *University of Missouri at Kansas City Law Review* 61 (3): 537–570.

Rosen, S. 1990. "Contracts and the Market for Executives." NBER Working Paper 3542. Washington, DC: National Bureau of Economic Research.

Rusk, J. 1993. "CEOs required to reveal salaries." *Globe and Mail* (Toronto), October 15, p. B1.

Shorten, R. 1992. "An Overview of the Revolt Against Executive Compensation." *Rutgers Law Review* 45 (1): 121–163.

Smith, A. [1776] 1937. *The Wealth of Nations*. Cannan edition. New York: Modern Library.

Stinson, M. 1993. "Executive pay disclosure wins diverse friends." *Globe and Mail* (Toronto), October 16, p. B1.

Tehranian H., and J. Waegelein. 1985. "Market Reaction to Short-Term Executive Compensation Plan Adoption." *Journal of Accounting and Economics* 7 (1–3): 131–144.

Trebilcock, M. 1994. *The Prospects for Reinventing Government*. Observation 38. Toronto: C.D. Howe Institute.

Vagts, D. 1983. "Challenges to Executive Compensation: For the Markets or For the Courts?" *Journal of Corporation Law* 8 (2): 231–276.

Comments, Part I

Is There a Problem with Executive Compensation?

Does Canada Have a Problem with Executive Compensation?

Martin F. Harts

Edward Iacobucci's paper outlines the economic theory of compensation for labor, examines legal constraints that affect executive compensation, considers empirical evidence about that compensation, and reviews current thinking in literature dealing with it. Much of the paper seems to imply that executive compensation levels in Canada are excessive; the "proof" includes US studies that deal with US executive compensation.

Is there a problem with executive compensation in Canada? As a compensation practitioner, I must answer that question with an unequivocal no. In a market economy, it is reasonable to expect that executives will try to charge what the traffic will bear for their own compensation. Is any compensation level, regardless of the amount, excessive if the market allows it to occur?

As a firm believer in the long-term wisdom of the market, I do not think Canadian executive compensation levels are problematic. Comparisons with executive pay in the United States and Europe suggest Canadian executives are a bargain. And the process of setting executive pay, particularly given the new openness created by mandated disclosure, will act as a moderating influence in the long term.

International Comparisons

Comparison of Canadian executive pay with that given in other countries, most notably the United States, Japan, and those in the

European Union, shows that Canada is a low-salary country. Comparing cash compensation for executives with organizations comparable in terms of sector and revenue size indicates that Canadian executives receive about 65 percent of what their US colleagues receive.

The executive compensation gap becomes very evident when a Canadian company looks to people from the United States, Germany, or France to fill an executive position in Canada. After taking cost-of-living differentials into account, executive talent from these countries usually will not consider a move at Canadian executive pay levels. An increasing number of Canadian companies that have transferred executives from the United States to Toronto, for example, have found that the only means of persuading them to relocate is to continue US compensation compensation levels and to pay them in US dollars. (Similar situations occur even for lower-level managers and some highly specialized technical personnel!) Conversely, the same companies have no difficulty in persuading Canadian executives to transfer to the United States, the United Kingdom, France, or Germany if the offer involves the local prevailing pay levels.

On the basis of international comparisons, therefore, one can hardly suggest that the absolute level of executive compensation in Canada is problematic or excessive.

The Process of Setting Executive Pay

Iacobucci's paper does not examine in great detail the impact on behavior that the disclosure regulations announced by the Ontario Securities Commission in October 1993 have had on the process of setting executive pay.

The chief executive officer (CEO) still gives the board annual recommendations for executive pay, but the dynamics between the players and the old assumptions have been challenged. No longer are the CEO's recommendations automatically approved by the compensation committee or the board. Recommendations to increase base pay are now usually backed up by market data, and, increasingly, base pay is being de-emphasized in favor of an annual bonus and long-term incentives. In other words, the potential upside in the "at risk" portion of pay is being promoted in the belief that compensation committees and, ultimately, the shareholders will be less likely to resist such adjustments.

The new disclosure rules are also changing the role of the annual bonus or incentive payments. Increasingly, compensation committees are requiring solid evidence in the form of quantitative performance criteria to justify bonuses. Paying executives incentives for performance at or in excess of targets is examined by institutional shareholders and the popular media in the context of company performance. Since the new rules came into force, compensation committee members are very sensitive to shareholders' questions about executive compensation at annual meetings.

This attitude, in itself, serves as a counterweight to outrageous compensation demands by executives in widely held corporations. In closely held corporations, those in which effective control of the company is in the hands of a single shareholder executive or family, the moderating influence of a compensation committee is clearly reduced. On balance, however, the openness that the new disclosure rules have brought to the process of setting executive compensation will serve to better protect the interests of shareholders than they have been in the past.

How Much Is Too Much?

In the past few years, the popular press has made much of the large "pay cheques" some executives receive. The media make little distinction among base salaries, annual bonuses, and money received by cashing in stock options.

In 1994, base salaries for the CEOs of Canadian corporations in the Toronto Stock Exchange 300 index averaged $407,000, with a median of $350,000. Adding in the annual bonuses increases total cash compensation for CEOs to an average of $632,000, with a median of $494,000. This level of cash compensation for CEOs of companies that had median revenues/sales of $586 million and average revenue/sales level of $1,511 million is not unreasonable.

The popular notion of sky-high compensation tends to arise from the amounts reported by executives who cash in on stock options. But is it unreasonable for a CEO to gain $5 million from cashing in options in a specific year? Such a payment is not an annual event, and it represents a benefit obtained only when the share price has increased significantly. One never hears any comments suggesting that the CEO's gain from exercising an option is made possible by a rise in the share price that also increases the wealth of shareholders. That message is conveniently forgotten by the media and the critics.

Conclusion

So I can only conclude that there is no problem with executive compensation. How much is too much? The market, with all its imperfections, is best equipped to answer that question. Certainly, an examination of executive compensation can turn up instances of abuse in the short term. But, over the longer term, especially given an increasingly global economy, the market will come closest to assigning the "correct" level to executive compensation.

Executive Compensation:
Some Comments on Why We Care

Robert D. Brown

Edward Iacobucci's paper appropriately raises and intelligently discusses virtually all of the important issues relating to the level and structure of executive compensation. It provides a comprehensive and well-organized overview of the economic and legal aspects of senior executive compensation, setting out not only a survey of the research but also some very thoughtful comments by the author.

It does, however, leave me wanting to make a few comments of my own about why the subject is important and some other issues.

Why Do We Care?

The first thing to ask in a discussion on executive compensation might be: Why do we care? Iacobucci's discussion, for all of its merits, is perhaps less than explicit in explaining why the amount that executives are paid is such an important issue in public policy terms and specifically why it is of such vital interest as to give rise to a number of imposing and, in some cases, frightening prescriptions for action.

Reasons for Concern

The issue, and most particularly the amount, of executive compensation is a matter of public debate and scrutiny for several reasons.

First, the amounts on occasion seem large and, therefore, to some, offensive to a sense of fairness. To see others treated far more generously than ourselves gives rise to very human feelings of jealousy, resentment, and possibly inadequacy. It is interesting that, in our society, this feeling of perceived excess seems primarily directed toward executives (and politicians' pension arrangements) and not toward other highly paid individuals. The salaries of football quarterbacks, basketball jumpers, and pop singers often dwarf the salaries of senior executives in Canada and equal those of the very highest paid executives in the United States.[1] But such enormous incomes do not seem to call forth the same feelings of envy and accountability that arise with respect to business compensation.

Second, and regardless of the level of executive compensation, the structure and the results frequently appear anomalous: virtue is not always rewarded, and sloth and incompetence occasionally appear to be exceptionally well compensated.

This anomaly exists, however, in many examples of compensation: those who have scarce skills, good unions, good agents, or jobs with highly profitable enterprises do better than those who do not. In 1995, the payroll of the Toronto Blue Jays, who finished last in their division, amounted to $42 million, considerably more than that of the Cleveland Indians, who finished first.[2]

Third, there is a perception — even a growing one — that the compensation system for senior executives is frequently inappropriate, in the sense that it does not encourage them to behave as they

1 The mass media report, for example, that each of the Beatles is expected to receive about US$100 million in royalties on a current re-issue of songs the group recorded more than 30 years ago, and Pete Best, a drummer dumped by the Beatles in 1962, will get up to US$10 million because he is in the background on one tape. Wayne Gretzky got US$1 million for a one-word Nike commercial, and Anne Murray is said to have earned C$25 million a year at her peak performance level.

2 Of course, I recognize the argument that individual Blue Jays are selling their services in a competitive environment without the possible conflicts that arise in setting executive compensation. The market for athletic and artistic services is far from perfect, however, and the conflict issue is not the first point in the public perception of business compensation.

should and thus does not provide the maximum effort for the cost. At a time when efficiency and competitiveness are the requirements of the day, there is a view that executive compensation cannot escape the rigors of re-engineering and restructuring.

Fourth, the divergence of interest between the owners of a corporation and the managers who actually run it results in a separation of ownership and control, raising a fundamental conflict in the setting of executive compensation.

One can argue that it is only the third and fourth issues above — defects in executive compensation methodology, and the inherent conflict in the setting of such compensation — that deserve further review. Yet, a good deal of the public commentary (not by Iacobucci but in the media) rests largely on the first two points — the size of the payments and the merits of the recipients.

Executive Compensation Practices Are Improving

As Iacobucci identifies, the situation with respect to executive compensation appears to be getting better. More market discipline in the compensation of chief executive officers (CEOs) of publicly held companies is being enforced by a combination of factors, including:

- higher competition in the market for execellent senior managers, which encourages greater efficiency in the use of such managers, and greater innovation and focus in their compensation schemes;
- an apparent strengthening of capital market disciplines, which means CEOs with weak records are more likely to be weeded out than in the past (Iacobucci might have made the point that the real issue with most CEOs who are not performing at the level of their compensation is not that their pay should be reduced but rather that their tenure should be questioned);
- increased disclosure of CEOs' compensation packages and the methodology used to set them — a change that is combining with improved corporate governance to gradually strengthen

both the structure of executive compensation and the oversight exercised by boards of directors; and

- increasing competition in the Canadian economy. As a result of the consequent drive for greater efficiency in all areas, many corporations have restructured their executive suites, not so much to diminish the compensation packages of the very top people but to reduce the number of highly paid senior managers. Many CEOs and other senior executives now operate with a greater span of control (a larger number of people and units reporting to them) than previously.

Additional Issues for Consideration

Iacobucci's analysis of a wide range of issues is both comprehensive and thoughtful, but I do want to mention some additional points.

First, Iacobucci may not have paid quite enough attention to the fact that many executive compensation schemes are now long term. In an increasing number of them, the payouts in any one period depend on performance or achievement over the previous two to six years. Accordingly, one can expect only an imperfect correlation of executive pay and perceived performance in the year in which a particular amount of compensation is reported.

A related point is that CEOs increasingly are expected to concentrate on the development and implementation of long-term strategies. In better-managed Canadian corporations, the emphasis, therefore, is not just on improving quarterly or annual results, but on the achievement of performance targets that can only be measured over a period of years — perhaps many years. It would be unfortunate if the discussion of executive performance led to a shortening of the focus of boards in setting compensation schemes or of executives in developing their strategies. A thoughtful CEO once told me that only several years after he had retired would his corporation find out whether or not he had done a good job. I think the remark was perceptive.

Second, and more fundamental, much of the analysis of the correlation of executive pay with corporate performance may be wide of the real point. One should not expect an executive's pay to be linked directly with current corporate profits; rather, in economic terms, executive remuneration should be correlated with his or her positive contribution to corporate performance — a measure that, in at least some cases, will not correspond to current corporate profitability (or even with short-term profitability measured against industry averages). For example, some three or four years ago, the board of directors of a pulp and paper company in the midst of the cyclical downturn in that industry could quite rationally have decided to pay its CEO a substantial bonus on the grounds that his or her stellar performance had prevented the company's substantial losses from turning into an even worse outcome. Similarly, in the current profitable upturn, the directors might, also quite rationally, decide not to award a bonus to an executive whom they did not believe had contributed something extra to that record. (Of course, basing executive bonuses on contributions to corporate goals requires informed judgment and is not susceptible of easy measurement from outside the organization.)

Third, as Iacobucci points out, the structure of executive compensation is perhaps even more important than the level. There are some interesting trends in this area: toward more long-term compensation arrangements (rather than short-term performance goals); toward, in a few cases, team goals and rewards in addition to, or even as a substitute for, individual incentive arrangements; and toward more complex or multilayer incentive plan packages to attempt to respond to all of the conflicting requirements noted in the paper.

Fourth, I found Iacobucci's comments on excessive board compensation slightly surprising. I agree that individual board members should not receive inappropriate bonuses, but the average compensation of directors in a number of companies may not be adequate to compensate properly the higher skills and attention now being demanded.

Finally, a company may have to pay a lot in order to attract the right people, regardless of how well it is doing at that moment. Consider, for example, that, when Air Canada wanted a CEO with relevant airline experience, it had to go to the United States. The individual chosen arrived with a mandate for reconstruction — a reconstruction that resulted in two years of the highest losses in the corporation's history — but Air Canada accepted that his performance could be judged only on a long-term basis if the company was to secure the talent it needed. An increasing number of corporations are price takers, not price setters, with respect to executive pay.

Overall, the structure of executive compensation is central to the efficiency of executive performance. Executive compensation policies should reinforce corporate strategy and add to corporate efficiency and effectiveness. But in an increasingly competitive and fast-paced world, it is not easy to provide plans that balance all of the complex and conflicting objectives; arrangements that do a top-notch job in one area — such as short-term corporate performance — may do damage in others. Inevitably, no single compensation structure is appropriate for all. Each package must be designed in relation to the strategy and goals of the individual corporation and to the influences a CEO can bring to bear on the achievement of those goals. The design of such systems requires value judgments, and individual corporations must act with considerable flexibility to find their own best fit.

Only in Canada...

A feature of Canada's economy not noted by Iacobucci is the fact that the great majority of its public companies — more than 70 percent — are not controlled by the public; rather, effective control rests with an individual or family, or the company is part of a larger corporate group.

This situation introduces some peculiarities to executive compensation in Canada that do not exist to the same extent in the United States or other countries in which the majority of public companies are, in fact, widely held. It is interesting that a number of the most highly paid CEOs in Canadian industry are, either individually or through family groups, in control of their enterprises. An examination of the broader implications of this fact would take one into some fascinating aspects of Canadian corporate culture.

Prescriptions Not Needed

Iacobucci discusses, but does not endorse, a number of draconian solutions to the executive compensation "problem," including the use of legal remedies and even tax legislation to influence the amount and structure of executive compensation. There are also suggestions for increased regulatory action.

I am firmly convinced that the last thing that would contribute to an improvement in Canadian corporate performance would be the introduction of regulations or even further enhanced disclosure with respect to executive pay. Incalculable harm could result from such heavy-handed intrusions into an area that rests so intensively on judgment and is so central to the achievement of corporate strategy. Here (and elsewhere), we do not need more regulation; what we need is sunshine, good sense, and flexibility.

To Sum Up

For better or worse, there is now substantially more disclosure not only of the amounts of executive compensation but also of its structure and justification. This information enables shareholders, particularly institutional ones, to have their own influence on compensation issues when these appear out of line. This sunlight is not without its cost, however. I am firmly convinced that the disclosure of executive compensation numbers over the past two years has materially increased average executive pay.[3]

In my view, two key changes would contribute to the further improvement of corporate performance through restructuring executive compensation.

3 In economic terms, wages are notoriously sticky with respect to downward adjustments, and any changes that induce convergence of salary levels are likely to involve harmonizing such payments at the top of the existing scale.

First, standards of corporate governance need to be increased, with a focus on having a board of directors with both the will and the means to form an independent judgment of management and its performance. As noted in the Toronto Stock Exchange's December 1994 report on corporate governance,[4] the standard for Canadian public corporations should be that

- a large majority of the board should be independent of the corporation and its senior officers;
- the board should heavily influence the appointment of new directors;
- the board should exercise an appropriate and informed oversight of management performance and the achievement of corporate strategy; and
- the board should have at its disposal the means (access to information, an appropriate committee structure, and an ability to influence agendas) to carry out its responsibilities independently of management.

Such independence in structure and operation can answer the fundamental conflict issue Iacobucci raises. I believe that corporate governance in Canada is improving and that one of the byproducts will be a more thoughtful review of executive compensation.

Second, there needs to be more study of the structure of executive compensation. To my mind, structure, rather than level, may be the area where attention should be focused. But again, designing appropriate incentive compensation schemes is extraordinarily difficult because of the need to balance conflicting objectives. The best results will be achieved through allowing corporations and their directors the right to exercise both flexibility and judgment.

I must also return to the question that I asked at the start of this comments: Why do we care? Reinforcing the importance of appropriate executive compensation is a further and broader issue: improving

4 Toronto Stock Exchange, Committee on Corporate Governance, *Where Were the Directors?* (Toronto, December 1994).

the public perception of the stewardship demonstrated by the leaders of the business community. It is important, not just for individual corporations but for the broad private sector, that corporations demonstrate that integrity and accountability are integral to basic corporate policy. In the long run, both the functioning of capital markets and the business community's contribution to public affairs depend on demonstrating to the public that business does manage its affairs appropriately in various areas, of which corporate compensation is one of the more prominent. In this broad sense, everyone should care that business appropriately discharges its responsibilities.

Where Is the Market Relationship?

Adam H. Zimmerman

Edward Iacobucci has ably reviewed executive compensation. In this comment, I will attempt to state a point of view, one that will probably not be popular with my former industrial colleagues, even though it is based on what I hope is an objective view of my long and varied experience, which has included posts as a senior official of a major company for 33 years, many directorships, and service on board committees on human resources.

The factor that probably most needs articulation is the lack of a marketplace for senior executives' salaries. People who are well placed in good jobs are usually happy with their lives and not looking to move around just for the sake of money. Moreover, executives in many industries are unlikely to have many opportunities to move. There is a theory, of course, that a good person can do anything. But experience suggests otherwise. Executives are not like professional athletes or movie stars. A good hockey player can play good hockey on any team — it is the same game — and good entertainers can presumably do their thing wherever they choose. On the other hand, a good insurance executive is not likely to be as good in the resources or the communications industry, any more than a resources industry or communications industry executive is likely to be a good insurance administrator. The reason is that the games are different; each industry has its own culture and its own requirements. The players are also different, and they all have different qualifications. Of course, I am generalizing, but I think that the record will support the view that the best executives stick to their own knitting.

Another important factor in the question of a marketplace for executives is its potential size. When involved in a search for a senior executive, one is invariably astonished both by the numbers of people available and by their quality. A recent search for which I was the chairman turned up at least five viable candidates, all of whom had substantial experience and reputation and none of whom would have been a high-risk choice. On the other hand, the chief executive officers (CEOs) of major companies cultivate the myth that it would be very hard to replace them.[1] Well they might propagate this fiction; if the veil is pierced, one would find many people of equal competence to take on the responsibilities.

The only real market for jobs in any industry comes at the lower end. A multitude of people are able to do most low-end jobs, and they often have some form of collective representation that ensures that fair wage levels are set and that the market cannot be used against the individual. Thus, one can argue that the whole structure should be built on market-based wages.

When salary administration was a relatively new thing, the relationship of each job to the others was clearly defined in terms of points convertible into dollars. The lowest level job was worth, say, 1,000 points, the next one 1,200, the next one 1,400, and so on. These relationships boiled down to limiting the step values to percentages of the lowest salary. At the top, the CEO might be paid something like 15 to 20 times the firm's lowest starting salary. Furthermore, the chief executive's salary would be no more than 50 percent higher than that of the number two person, and so on down the pole.

With the legislated publication of salaries, however, the race was on. Every company was anxious to show that it paid well and that its executives were doing as well as the competition's. Iacobucci quotes Crystal as reporting that most firms claim to paying their

1 Indeed, I should not restrict this to comment to CEOs. I am sure it applies to big-time executives at every level.

executives in the top one or two quartiles (which leaves one wondering who pays in the bottom quartiles). Of course, the result has been a vast inflation of salaries to the ridiculous levels that are now extant.

Fortunately, some sense is beginning to come into this picture as boards realize that million-dollar salaries do not sit well, particularly when companies may not be doing very well. Thus, we get into the whole realm of performance-based salaries: something like 50 to 60 percent of total compensation can be offered in the form of incentive bonuses or options, which are awarded in accord with the fortunes of the company. The difficulty, however, is that, in some industries, the best management in the world cannot improve the results during a down cycle.[2] Some companies in this situation take the view that, even though the executives will do badly in a down year, they will do extraordinarily well in an up year.[3] The folly of this approach has been well exhibited by one major corporate group, which believed that executives should be paid heavily in share ownership or stock options and found that the system failed mightily.

To come back to where I began, I do not believe that top executive salaries are any longer set according to a rational system. They are not market related, nor are they related to the remuneration of the lower ranks in the same organization. The perfect schemes for paying executives according to performance remain to be developed, but at least the move is on, and undoubtedly some sense will finally come into the equation.

2 This situation is particularly common in Canada, whose economy is so heavy with resources industries and all of their cyclicality.

3 One problem is that of timing: people may retire at a low end of the cycle and thus forgo any possibility of the lush rewards of good years.

Some Real-World Complexities

John D. McNeil

Edward Iacobucci's excellent paper provides a methodical examination of the issues in executive compensation from both an economic and a legal perspective. Analysis that is firmly based in economic theory has the advantage of running along a logical path. It is thus difficult to disagree with most of Iacobucci's broad conclusions. The only reservations I have concern the completeness and realism of the underlying premises. The world as we find it is obviously a good deal more complicated than the analysis suggests.

Capital-Intensive, Cyclical Industries

The following example, based on my own brief experience as a railway analyst some 30 years ago, may serve to muddy the waters of crystal-clear analysis.

A railway that had been cobbled together in a series of nineteenth-century speculations was experiencing less-than-satisfactory economics. The management decided to diversify and, accordingly, it acquired businesses that manufactured boots, shoes, clothes, and luggage, distributed liquor, and expanded into a variety of other activities.

These businesses did quite well and, after some time, interested investment bankers suggested that shareholder value would be enhanced if the company did not own a railway. The management agreed, but it did not sell the railway; rather, it was spun off to the existing shareholders!

One wonders what the directors of the newly independent railway discussed at their first meeting. Probably they did not discuss diversification as a strategy because thereafter the company stuck to railroading.

The moral of this story is that somebody has to own the railway, and somebody has to manage it.

An addendum is that, at that time, railways earned decidedly low rates of return on invested capital. Each year they retained and reinvested substantial amounts of earnings, but the rate of return on the enlarged investment remained more or less constant. The explanation I received for this apparently irrational behavior was that a failure to reinvest would lead to a large decline in earnings. In other words, while the average rate of return on invested capital remained low, the marginal return was, in fact, extremely high.

It seemed to me at the time that the loyalty of railroad managers was to the enterprises they served, rather than to the shareholders of those enterprises. Inasmuch as somebody had to own the railway, one cannot say they were wholly wrong. Furthermore, the stock market of the day seemed to fairly value the companies in accordance with their indifferent prospects. It is worth noting, however, that, in the fullness of time, the industry was substantially deregulated, and those who had stuck to their business prospered mightily.

Railways are an extreme example of businesses with large amounts of sunk investment. Steel, paper, machinery, automobile manufacturers, and mining companies are also characterized by huge sums of immobile capital. Another feature common to such businesses is that their results are much influenced by factors external to the firm. Iacobucci deals with this problem, speaking of "the imperfect correlation between executive effort and firm performance" (p. 15). The suggested solution of using comparative performance measures based on the construction of a peer group will often prove impractical. It is hard to tell the workers on the shop floor (or the shareholders, for that matter) that the senior executives earned worthwhile bonuses because, on a relative basis, the firm lost less money than its competitors.

In summary, the theory gives imperfect guidance on how to compensate executives in capital-intensive, cyclical businesses. One might argue that, since they have so little control over the firm's destiny, it is pointless to give them any incentive compensation. Equally, one might argue that effective management of such enterprises requires such high levels of skill, energy, and dedication that it calls for high levels of compensation, in one form or another.

What Motivates Managers?

The economic analysis in the paper presents a decidedly one-sided picture of what motivates a manager. In dealing with the question of agency costs, Iacobucci says (p. 12):

> A properly framed compensation contract can lower the private benefit of engaging in a particular undesirable activity, increase the private benefit of engaging in desirable activities and/or increase the cost to the executive of engaging in suboptimal behavior.

And a little later (p. 19): "An executive who is paid strictly by salary is more likely to shirk and consume other perks rather to than engage in utility-reducing hard work." I suppose the key words in the last sentence are "more likely." My guess is, not by enough to be of any significance (though I agree that such a method of compensation will lead the executive to take less risk, which may not be a bad thing in certain businesses).

Thus, while one may appreciate the rigor of the analysis, one is left to wonder whether this model of the executive with Pavlovian responses solely to pecuniary benefits is not so extreme as to be a potential source of error. Managers do not respond solely to the carrot of money and the stick of being fired. Ambition, a sense of achievement, loyalty to an institution, and a sense of duty are but a few examples of other powerful influences on managerial behavior.

Iacobucci confirms that research finds only "modest links between performance and executive pay" (p. 33). Given my earlier observations about capital-intensive and cyclical businesses and any business whose prospects can be radically altered by external events, I do not find this empirical conclusion surprising.

In discussing the growth in executive pay, Iacobucci notes that it has far outstripped the growth in pay of other occupations and the growth in earnings in the Standard and Poor's 500. Perhaps stock market appreciation provides a benchmark that is more relevant and explanatory than earnings growth. For example, between December 1979 and December 1989, the S & P Index rose 227.5 percent. Between 1982 and the present, the Dow Jones Industrial Index has increased fivefold. In brief, stock market performance, which significantly influences executive pay (through share options and similar incentives), has been extraordinarily favorable during this time. By contrast, the Dow Jones Industrial Average was essentially flat between 1972 and 1982. Who knows what it may do during the next decade?

The rise in executive pay may also reflect the increasing demands of the job. Government relations, taxation, regulation, litigation, environmental standards, governance issues, and generally higher expectations of firms' being good corporate citizens are arguably much greater challenges than they were in previous decades.

It is also worth noting that much of the author's evidence is taken from US examples. I believe that the cultural differences between the United States and Canada are substantial enough to invalidate at least some conclusions across the border.

When it comes to other international comparisons, firm conclusions are difficult to draw since the data are very imperfect. Are the job descriptions of chief executives in different countries really the same? For example, Japanese executives operating in a collegial, consensus-seeking style may be burdened with less individual accountability than their counterparts in other countries. At a conference on corporate governance,[1] a Japanese executive asked, "Are you telling me that the board of directors has a greater duty to an institution that purchased the shares two months ago and plans to

1 The Ditchley Conference on Corporate Governance, held at Ditchley Park, England, April 24–26, 1992.

sell them next week than to an employee who has provided 30 years of loyal service?" The attitude reflected in that question (which I think is a very good one) may account for the discount in Japanese executive compensation.

In examining the empirical evidence, Iacobucci describes the remarkable case of Disney executive Michael Eisner, who took home $203 million in 1993. This astronomical sum provokes several simple-minded questions:

- If Eisner had had a significantly less lucrative contract, would Disney have performed less well?
- If Eisner had had a significantly more lucrative contract, would Disney have performed even better?
- How many other people, having received Eisner's contract, could have duplicated his performance?
- Would Eisner's performance have been as stellar if he had had a similar contract but been asked to run a totally different business?

It appears that Disney's performance sprang from the happy confluence of the person, the business, and the time.

Still speaking of Eisner's remuneration, Iacobucci says, "It is difficult for an analyst to conclude that such a sum is excessive" (p. 31). I think it is possible to argue, however, that the Disney directors who gave Eisner his contract did not fully understand the business or appreciate the potential of the company. In other words, I think that Eisner would have run just as hard for a good deal less money.

On the other hand, it is worth noting that wealth can alter behavior and that making an executive enormously rich can lead to a diversion of his or her energies and attention.

Conclusion

The commentators on the Iacobucci paper were asked, Is there a problem with executive compensation? At present, a company's directors determine management compensation and, in the case of the five highest-paid managers of a public company, the information is disclosed. I am hard pressed to think of a better method. The search for the "right" formula for setting executive pay is likely to have as little success as medieval scholars' search for a "just price." Iacobucci's leads this reader to conclude that shareholders, directors, and managers should avoid prescriptive rules and be prepared to deal with individual cases on their own merits.

Comments, Part II

If There Is a Problem, What Are Its Causes?

How Can We Solve the Problems of Executive Compensation?

Austin C. Beutel

My experience as a securities analyst, investor, and company director confirms the statement in Edward Iacobucci's overview that "there is no simple economic optimum for a compensation package in all situations" (p. 47). Furthermore, I would add emphatically, there is no optimum compensation package for a corporation's senior executives that survives unaltered for more than a few years; changes are bound to occur because of changes in some or all of the following: corporate fortunes, strategic objectives, management personnel, tax laws, and competitive compensation practices.

It is important for us to keep in mind, even though the press may not, that the relationship of owners and executives is a critical factor in many Canadian companies. Control over the selection of board members[1] typically creates an environment for the existence of a special relationship between the chief executive officer (CEO) and the board, which is legally charged with setting compensation.

Problems

The problem with executive compensation is twofold. The first and most important issue is public reaction. There is a perception in the

1 Consider, for example, the situation at Seagram (because of significant ownership), at Magna (because of multiple-voting capitalization), and at Canadian banks (because of ownership constraints).

community at large — among some shareholders and other interested and disinterested observers — that executive compensation, particularly of CEOs, is too high, even though different companies and different executives may appear on the "ten best paid" list from year to year. That this perception of excessive compensation exists is clear from the multitude of commentaries from the press, financial analysts, and institutional shareholders. The perception is also a reality because it is not good business (or good politics) for the corporate sector to be seen as paying salaries that are progressively higher in absolute terms and in relative terms compared with those of other workers when the country has static (or declining) living standards, persistent high unemployment, and inconsistent corporate results.

The second issue, which is internal, concerns the method of setting executive compensation. Many corporations reportedly base compensation on competitive considerations — what Iacobucci refers to as relative compensation — but these comparisons are not necessarily thorough, reliable, or appropriate. The evidence for this second problem is largely anecdotal, based on personal experience. Recent moves to place performance evaluation and compensation in independent compensation committees are to be applauded, but it would be naive to believe that compensation strategy is independent of the CEO in most companies.

The structure of an incentive compensation program and the risk proportion of total compensation should reflect corporate strategy and the stage of the company's development or maturity. These features then determine the characteristics of the executive needed. This is often not the case.

What Causes the Problems?

Theorists envision effective board functioning as a consensual process in which the directors work in a collegial, nonconfrontational environment as they seek to enhance shareholder worth. Such conditions foster the coming together of people of similar values and lead to interlocking or dependent relationships that make it easy to rationalize a broad range of acceptable performance and compensation, especially when the economic consequences of such determinations are not concentrated on any one shareholder.

The corporate form tends to separate ownership and control. Many boards make efforts (which I support) to compensate for that separation and align executives with the interests of shareholders by including a variable component in compensation. This approach sets the stage for a situation in which total compensation in any one year bears little or no relationship (or an exaggerated relationship) to the corporation's actual success during that year. In other words, the exercise of options and/or the sale of shares acquired through options and stock purchase plans produce compensation that may be out of sync with reported earnings, share prices, and dividends, which are the usual measures of success in the shareholders' eyes.

Furthermore, the part of executive compensation that involves high cash proceeds diverts executive attention to personal investment and reinvestment challenges and away from the employer's interests.

The empirical evidence, according to Iacobucci, supports the perception that executive reward is not symmetrical — that is, good performance is rewarded but poor performance, however assessed, is not often punished quickly enough. Admittedly, starting salaries for newly hired or newly promoted CEOs are based on negotiation, often with the assistance of compensation experts, but with the passage of time, companies tend to build on these foundations without re-examining the basic premises. This problem of changing conditions may continue for a few years but cannot persist in any individual company indefinitely. Competitive conditions, moral considerations, and the responsibility of corporate directors to fulfill their legal obligation to enhance shareholder value usually leads to dismissal for poor performance or vulnerability to acquisition.

Meanwhile, however, executive compensation may skyrocket. The new disclosure requirements, in my view, have had a greater impact in forcing a race-to-the-top mentality than in promoting restraint out of embarrassment.

What Are the Appropriate Responses?

The problems with executive compensation call for a variety of policy responses. The following recommendations are designed to deal with both the external and internal problems, identified above, by removing the focus of attention from the compensation of executives (especially CEOs), which is only a minor element in corporate assessment, and by providing for a better alignment of directors' and shareholders' interests without impinging on directors' flexibility to perform their responsibilities.

- Eliminate the now-mandatory disclosure of executive salaries. Shareholders elect boards to serve as their representatives in overseeing management. Shareholders do not appoint CEOs, nor do they set salary levels. That is the board's job. Providing shareholders — and thus the public, peers, and competitors — with CEO compensation information is no better way to help them judge the performance of the company, its board, or its CEO than letting them know how much the company is paying for product distribution, raw materials, or legal services. Such information may provide oglers with vicarious pleasure or envy or dissidents with ammunition. But shareholders, who are the ones who elect the board, should judge the performance of their representatives and their investment on the basis of corporate profitability and other absolute or relative benchmarks (including stock quotations, where applicable). Institutional investors, who, because of the size of their holdings, may suffer from reduced liquidity, should be prepared to serve on corporate boards and be bound by board confidentiality and the trading restrictions that implies. The notion that major investors should have access or influence without commensurate responsibility goes against standards of fairness.
- Change taxation policies so that stock options are taxed not when they are exercised but when the shares acquired through options are disposed of. If we believe in a market economy and

the rewards of enterprise, attempting to align the interests of a senior executive entrusted with the management of the corporation's resources to that of its shareholders makes eminent sense. That is what stock options try to do, and the benefits of such rewards should be taxed on realization, just as other benefits are taxed, and not at acquisition.

- Provide shareholders the opportunity to vote for individual directors, rather than for a slate in its entirety. Thus, if a shareholder wishes to exercise his or her disapproval of executive salaries, of the continuing employment of certain executives, or of particular directors, that shareholder may vote against selected nominees.
- Require that directors receive at least 50 percent of their compensation in shares of the corporation, rather than in cash, to align their interests more closely with those of the shareholders whom they represent.
- Provide that directors be elected for a period of three years, on a staggered basis, to give them an additional element of independence. Most directors serve for much longer, so the question of stability and continuity is not an issue. All directors' terms should, however, expire automatically on a change of control.
- Provide that boards of directors consist entirely of independent persons, except that the CEO may be a member of the board.

Executive Compensation: The Importance of Context

Jeffrey G. MacIntosh

The popular press is full of stories about excessive remuneration. Some of this reporting is attributable to reporters' (and the general public's) ignorance of compensation theory and practice.[1] That excesses exist is unquestionable, however, and should not be surprising. No principal-agent system can be invented that is free of abuse. Iacobucci rightly argues that we should not rest our judgment about the adequacy of the system of corporate compensation (or, more generally, corporate governance) on an analysis of pathological cases. What is important is the *frequency* of such cases, whether compensation appears to do its intended job in the *average* case, and (most important) whether any particular form of regulatory intervention would be cost effective (see MacIntosh 1994a). Moreover, particular schemes must be assessed in particular contexts.

Agency Costs and Market Context

Properly used, executive compensation can be a way of containing or limiting management agency costs. Its utility must, however, be considered in context. How effective are other devices at accomplishing this end? In particular, how well do product, capital, and control markets work in disciplining management? The better these markets work, the less the need for pay-for-performance schemes to motivate management.

1 This point is made forcefully by Murphy (1995).

The strength of these other markets can vary markedly over time. Two illustrations from the United States are instructive. First, the advent of "poison pills" in 1982 and the proliferation of state anti-takeover statutes greatly blunted the efficacy of the takeover market in providing managerial discipline.[2] One might thus conjecture that managements were less disciplined in the late 1980s and early 1990s than in the 1970s or early 1980s (although the 1980s also witnessed the dramatic emergence of institutional investor voice, perhaps partly in response to the blunting of the takeover device as a disciplinary tool). But takeovers and compensation can be viewed as substitute devices for disciplining management, so the reduction in the number of takeovers may well account for some of the increase in compensation observed in this period (although some evidence suggests that rapid increases in executive compensation are a worldwide phenomenon — see, for example, "Nice Work," *The Economist*, December 10, 1994, p. 67; Abowd and Bognanno 1995).

Second, a comparison of the compensation of chief executive officers (CEOs) in the United States in the 1930s and 1980s (Jensen and Murphy 1990b) finds lower average pay in the 1980s, accompanied by lesser (and surprisingly low) pay/performance sensitivity.[3] Since there appear to have been fewer market controls over management misbehavior in the 1930s than in the 1980s,[4] both findings may be a natural product of the maturing of various market controls and the commensurately declining need to use compensation schemes to motivate managers.[5]

2 The collapse of the junk bond market at the end of the 1980s further contributed to the blunting of the takeover as a disciplinary tool, although this market has since revived.

3 Leonard (1990, 21–S) also finds a low pay/performance sensitivity.

4 Takeovers and proxy contests were all but unheard of in the 1930s. Institutional investors hardly existed. The Berle and Means "management controlled corporation" (in which managers were subject to little or no effective discipline from shareholders) was at its zenith.

5 As Iacobucci indicates, a heightened pay/performance sensitivity should lead to an increase in total management compensation because of managerial risk aversion.

The Need for Empirical Study

Iacobucci nicely summarizes the theory of compensation. I stress one vitally important point: there is no *theoretically* optimal compensation package. As Holmstrom pointed out as early as 1979, considerations of efficient risk bearing dictate that an executive receive a fixed salary (Holmstrom 1979). Where the principal (the shareholders) cannot directly observe the actions of the agent (the manager), however, the manager will be tempted to cheat on effort or to engage in the other forms of agency costs Iacobucci outlines. For this reason, it is necessary to introduce an incentive component into the agent's compensation. By themselves, however, incentive considerations dictate that the managers receive *no* fixed salary; their pay should be fully contingent on performance.[6]

Thus, theory alone cannot set the optimal balance between efficient risk sharing and the need to optimize executive incentives. This indeterminacy places a premium on empirical studies of the relationship between firm performance and alternative forms of pay. Only by studying what actually works in practice can one determine what is optimal.

Low Pay/Performance Sensitivity

Jensen and Murphy (1990b) comprehensively review compensation arrangements for the CEOs of large US public corporations. They argue that, despite the inability of pure theory to generate a real-world solution to the tradeoff between incentive and risk sharing, the observed pay/performance sensitivity is consistent only with unrealistically high levels of risk aversion. This leads Jensen and Murphy to suggest that executive compensation arrangements are not doing what principal-agent theory suggests they should do: motivate executives to maximize firm value.

6 The ideal would include negative as well as positive realizations — that is, in some states of the world, the executive should compensate the corporation. Wealth constraints prevent this desideratum.

Haubrich, however, demonstrates theoretically that small degrees of executive risk aversion may dictate an extremely low pay/performance sensitivity, and that even this very low degree of pay/performance sensitivity may "provide incentives and substantially increase the value of the firm" (1994, 275). These are important theoretical results and suggest that a low pay/performance sensitivity is not inconsistent with principal-agent theories of executive compensation.

Stock Options

Iacobucci notes that stock options may give executives an incentive to take on risky projects, even though these projects are not the best available to the company, in order to increase the value of their options. To the extent that executives receive part of their pay as fixed salary, however, their incentive is to do exactly the opposite: to choose low-risk projects even though these are not the best available to the company (see Coffee 1986; Smith and Watts 1982).[7]

Again, as a matter of pure theory, it is impossible to tell how to trade off fixed salary and incentive compensation so that the executives will adopt the best projects (those with the highest net present value) regardless of their level of risk.

The Nirvana Fallacy

No compensation scheme is perfect. Although "pay for performance" has become a mantra for experts in corporate compensation, all incentive schemes are flawed in some respect. For example, many corporations pay short- or long-term incentive compensation based on accounting earnings (or other accounting variables).[8] Managers

---

7 Note that this argument does not depend on the executives' being underdiversified, although underdiversification increases the incentive to invest only in low-risk projects.

8 Leonard found that 98.3 percent of the corporations in his random sample had short-term bonus schemes in place in 1985, and 97.2 percent had long-term plans (1990, 25-S and 26-S).

are well situated to influence the choice of accounting techniques, however, and will often do so if this results in an increase in reported earnings (see Healy 1985).[9]

Both accounting-based schemes and those based on share prices are also imperfect because, as Iacobucci notes, compensation is then influenced by factors other than managerial performance.

It is also important to note that managers work in *teams*. It is thus difficult to design a compensation package that rewards *individual* performance.[10]

In short, no pay package is without flaws. Thus, the identification of a flaw in a particular compensation scheme is hardly an overwhelming objection to that type of scheme. What this emphasizes, once again, is that empirical assessment is vital in evaluating executive pay packages.

The Importance of Stock Ownership

Most studies examining the pay/performance relationship ignore stock ownership. This practice is perilous. It is clear from empirical studies of executive compensation in the United States (for example, Jensen and Murphy 1990b; Murphy 1985; Benston 1985) that, historically, the greatest performance incentive has come not from bonuses, options, or other incentive devices, but from stock ownership. Ignoring such ownership can yield misleading results in both longitudinal and cross-sectional studies.

In their pathbreaking work on agency costs, Jensen and Meckling (1976) posit an essentially linear relationship between managerial stock ownership and agency costs. Thus, as management ownership increases, one should observe better alignment of manager and shareholder interests and less need for incentive compensation. In

9 A particularly egregious example may be found in the 1976 New York Supreme Court case decision of *Kamin v. American Express Co.*

10 On the agency difficulties created by production in teams, see, generally, Alchian and Demsetz (1972).

fact, studies on the relationship between managerial share ownership and firm value (Morck, Shleifer, and Vishny 1988; McConnell and Servaes 1990; Wruck 1988) suggest that a nonlinear relationship exists between managerial ownership and firm value, and that this arises because increasing management ownership does more than merely align manager and shareholder interests: it also gives managers the ability to entrench themselves in office. Over certain ranges of ownership (which may differ for different sizes of corporations), the entrenchment effect appears to dominate the alignment effect. Thus, increasing stock ownership may result in nonlinear changes to compensation packages (see Lambert, Larcker, and Weigelt 1993[11]).

Other Observations

A few more observations on the theory and practice of executive compensation follow.

Firm-Specific Human Capital

An executive of a firm that specializes in one product, especially a unique product, has a large amount of specialized human capital tied up in the firm. The higher the degree of an executive's asset specificity, the worse the individual's prospects outside the firm and the greater the cost of job loss. For risk-averse executives, one would expect this prospectively heightened cost to be compensated by the payment of larger total compensation.

Although there is some evidence that asset specificity is not an important factor in the setting of executive compensation (Leonard 1990; Finkelstein and Hambrick 1988), the subject is worth further investigation. Of particular interest is whether asset specificity has increased over time. If it has, it might lend support to Jensen and Murphy's view that inefficient "implicit regulation" (1990b, 36)

11 Although the authors find that, as managerial ownership goes up, managerial compensation goes down, they did not test for a nonlinear relationship.

accounts for the reduction in real pay between the 1930s and the 1980s (since, in the face of increased executive specialization, real pay should have, *ceteris paribus*, gone up and not down). Increasing asset specificity is also one explanation for apparent run-ups in executive salaries in the past ten years, during which corporate "focus" (product specialization) has become as much a governance mantra as "pay for performance."

Financing Decisions

Iacobucci notes that the compensation package may affect executives' selection of investment projects. It may also affect their financing decisions. Smith and Watts (1982), for example, note that in some cases a bonus may not be paid unless earnings reach a stated portion of equity and/or long-term debt. In such cases, executives have an incentive not to increase the amount of equity or long-term debt but to finance the firm with short-term debt and leases, even if the latter course is not in the best interests of the firm.

The Overretention Problem

A common manifestation of agency costs is managerial overretention of earnings (that is, managers' failure to pay dividends when the only projects available have a negative net present value).[12] Smith and Watts (1982, 149) argue that, since managers may overretain earnings in order to increase the likelihood of being paid, compensation plans should — and in practice frequently do — address the overretention problem.

Financial Reporting

Accounting-based incentive schemes give management an incentive to influence the choice of accounting techniques (Healy 1985). Many

12 Indeed, managerial overretention is the basis for Jensen's "free cash flow" theory of corporate takeovers as well as one explanation of the virtues of corporate debt (in addition to the payment of dividends). (See Jensen 1986; Easterbrook 1984.)

studies, however, indicate that changes in accounting techniques do not result in mistaken market valuations of the firm (see Ross and Westerfield 1988, 315–317). Thus, although accounting-based incentive schemes may result in changes in accounting methods, they do not appear to result in materially less informative financial reporting.

Assessing the Empirical Record

Iacobucci cites studies (Brickley, Bhagat, and Lease 1985; Tehranian and Waegelein 1985) that show a positive relationship between share price and the adoption of both short- and long-term incentive compensation schemes. These studies are helpful, but their results should be used with some caution. Increases in share price following adoption of an incentive pay package can be attributed to at least three different factors: a market judgment that executives will be better motivated; anticipated corporate tax savings; or interpretation of plan adoption as a signal that superior performance lies on the horizon.

Miller and Scholes (1982) demonstrate that most US equity-based incentive compensation schemes have tax advantages for the firm (see also Smith and Watts 1982). In neither study cited by Iacobucci are the authors able to determine how much of the positive stock market reaction was attributable to tax savings. In a study separate from the one Iacobucci cites, however, Bhagat, Brickley, and Lease test the stock market impact of the adoption of compensation plans that do not yield tax savings to the corporation. They find a positive reaction of 4.72 percent, providing evidence that "compensation schemes that include shares of common stock can, at least in some circumstances, increase shareholder wealth for reasons other than reducing taxes" (1985, 206).

Moreover, Smith and Watts suggest that in many cases the tax benefits can be achieved without using incentive plans. They conclude that "tax effects are at best a partial explanation for the nature, existence and growing popularity of incentive plans" (1982, 153).

A final, more troublesome reason for caution in interpreting studies of this nature is that the stock market reaction may reflect the informational content of adopting the plan rather than the merits of the plan itself. Managers may use their power to encourage adoption of an incentive plan when they know that the firm is headed for banner performance. If so, then adoption of an incentive plan signals the market that it should expect abnormally good performance, driving up the price.

Tehranian and Waegelein (1985) find a positive share price reaction to adoptions of short-term incentive programs (abstracting from market movements) that averaged 11 percent. They could not, however, determine if this rise was directly attributable to the plans adopted or the signaling effect of adoption. Indeed, in the period from six months before the announcement to the announcement date, the share price increase averaged about 20 percent, indicating that, in many of the sample firms, unexpectedly good performance occurred *prior* to the adoption of the plan.

Other studies finding share price run-ups in connection with the adoption of incentive plans suffer from the same inability to distinguish incentive and signaling effects. This counsels some caution in interpreting the results. For example, Bhagat, Brickley, and Lease say:

> Given our sample and data, distinguishing completely between incentive and signalling arguments for explaining the market reaction to stock purchase plans is impossible. We interpret the evidence as supporting the position that incentive effects are an important motivation for these plans. However, as the two effects are not mutually exclusive, it is possible that both effects are important. (1985, 208.)

Cross-Country Comparisons

The importance of market context has frequently been overlooked not only in longitudinal studies of corporate compensation but in cross-country comparisons as well. Straight comparisons of compensation may be somewhat misleading if they ignore differences in the relative strengths of market disciplinary devices in different countries.

Because of the institutional structure of the markets in Germany and Japan, for example, these countries have fewer hostile takeovers than does the United States, but they have relatively more corporations with a controlling shareholder. These factors may affect the marginal utility of pay/performance schemes.[13]

Canada has fewer restrictions on hostile takeovers than the United States[14] and most Canadian companies are dominated by a controlling shareholder (Daniels and MacIntosh 1991). Both these factors may well lead to a higher probability that nonperforming executives will be promptly removed, which, in turn, may de-emphasize the need for pay-for-performance schemes to motivate management.[15] Although this insight is only the start of an analysis, it again illustrates the importance of context.

---

13 Kaplan's study of the compensation practices of large Japanese and US corporations suggests that there is little difference in the relationship between performance and pay in the two countries. Similarly, there appears to be little difference in the relationship between performance and the probability of dismissal. Yet Japanese executives own only about half as much stock and stock options in their corporations and should be less motivated than US executives to maximize shareholder profits. Kaplan suggests, however, that "[o]ne possible explanation [for the lower managerial shareholdings in Japan] is that closer monitoring by main banks and large corporate shareholders in Japan partially offsets the higher managerial incentives provided by shareholdings in the United States" (1994, 513).

14 Although poison pills finally came to this country in 1989, Canada has no analogue to the anti-takeover statutes of many US states. Moreover, Canadian securities regulators and courts have closely policed the use of poison pills by management. (See MacIntosh and Schwartz 1995.)

15 In fact, Magnan, St-Onge, and Thorne (1995) find lower levels of CEO pay in Canadian-controlled companies than in widely held firms, although they also find that the presence of a controlling shareholder has a larger impact in the United States than in Canada. They also find that the relationship between stock market returns and CEO compensation is weaker for closely held firms than for widely held ones. Curiously, Elitzur and Halpern (1995) find *higher* compensation in controlled than in widely held companies. They also find evidence that the relationship between stock market return and compensation is *stronger* in controlled companies. It is worth noting that, although Magnan, St-Onge, and Thorne restrict their sample to interlisted companies, Elitzur and Halpern do not.

Iacobucci rightly points out another limitation on cross-country comparisons: in many countries, compensation is often hidden, by being paid in perquisites or by other means.[16]

More General Comments

Other land mines lurk in cross-country comparisons. They include the following:

- Marginal tax rates vary substantially from one country to another. In a fully integrated international market for executives, one would expect equalization of *after-tax* incomes. Yet comparison studies are almost always made in *before-tax* dollars, so they can mislead (see Abowd and Bognanno 1995).
- Purchasing power varies from one country to another. For example, large houses in Sao Paulo may be cheaper than large houses in San Francisco. Because comparable pay packages equate managerial utility, rather than total cash consideration, differences in purchasing power must be taken into account whenever possible.
- Executives in different countries may place different values on pecuniary and nonpecuniary compensation.[17] An article in *Forbes* (Morais, Eisenstodt, and Kichen 1993), for example, claims that Japanese executives value the prestige of an executive position more than their US counterparts and are thus willing to accept lower pecuniary remuneration.

16 Some German companies, for example, pay more than one salary: one in Germany and another in a tax haven. The latter is often not reported. (See Morais, Eisenstodt, and Kichen 1993.) The same source indicates that a 1992 Towers Perrin study finds that Mexican and Brazilian CEOs earn the highest cash compensation in the world.

17 Indeed, the point can be generalized: because of cultural differences, executives may derive different utilities from either the cash or the noncash features of the compensation package.

- Compensation and job security are substitutes. Executives in some countries may accept less cash compensation in return for greater job security.[18] Few studies take the probability of dismissal into account in examining executive pay.[19]
- Executive stock ownership varies from country to country.[20] Stock ownership has historically been the most important source of wealth/performance sensitivity (at least in the United States). Significant stock ownership may make it unnecessary to motivate executives with incentive compensation schemes. Thus, differences in stock ownership need to be taken into account before one can pronounce upon the relative efficacy of the pay/performance relationship in different countries.
- Another control variable is the presence of institutional shareholders or other large blockholders, who are more effective than retail shareholders in monitoring management. Indeed, Mehran finds evidence that the larger the percentage of a firm's shares held by outside blockholders, the lower the proportion of an executive's equity-based compensation, "suggesting that moni-

---

18 It is often suggested that Japanese executives have greater security of tenure (see, for example, Morais, Eisenstodt, and Kichen 1993). Kaplan (1994), however, finds little difference in the probability of dismissal for poor performance between large US and Japanese corporations. Indeed, he finds evidence that Japanese executives are *more* likely than their US counterparts to be dismissed when the firm's earnings are negative.

A number of studies find that poor performance elevates the probability of CEO dismissal. See, for example, Warner, Watts, and Wruck (1988); Weisbach (1988); and Coughlan and Schmidt (1985). Jensen and Murphy (1990b) confirm this relationship; however, they point out that, although poor performance elevates the probability of dismissal, dismissal remains an extremely low probability event. They also point out that golden parachutes considerably lessen the cost of dismissal for the executive. Vancil (1987) estimates that 80 percent of departing CEOs retain a seat on the board of directors and 36 percent continue to serve as its chair. This evidence is inconsistent with the claim made by Linden and Rotenier (1994). During recent years, however, the probability of dismissal may well have increased.

19 There are some exceptions, such as Kaplan (1994) and Jensen and Murphy (1990b); the latter, however, focuses only on the US market.

20 Kaplan (1994) finds that Japanese executives own roughly half as much stock in their firms as do US executives. The latter also hold more stock options.

toring by outside blockholders may be a substitute for incentive pay for executives" (1995, 163).[21]

- The presence of outside directors on a board of directors may operate as a discipline independent of compensation schemes, making it less necessary to use incentive pay to motivate managers. It should be noted, however, that Mehran (1995) finds that the more outside directors, the more an executive's pay is received in the form of equity-based compensation.[22] This evidence suggests that a full explanation of differences in compensation practices between countries should take board compensation into account.
- Average company size varies from one country to another. Since there is robust evidence that compensation increases with size (see, for example, Jensen and Murphy 1990b; Murphy 1985, 32; Baker 1988; Kostiuk 1990),[23] cross-country comparisons need to be adjusted for corporate size to be truly meaningful.
- Compensation practices vary from one industry to another (see, for example, Gerhart and Milkovich 1990), perhaps because of different degrees of industry risk or different levels of executive task specialization. Since sectoral concentrations vary from one country to another (Canada, for example, has a high concentra-

21 Curiously, however, Mehran finds no statistically significant relationship between firm performance and the holdings of outside blockholders, including individuals, institutions, and corporations. He suggests that this is because some blockholders monitor effectively while others do not, muddying the results (1995, 180–181).

22 Curiously, although Mehran finds that greater equity-based pay increases firm value, he also finds that board composition is unrelated to firm performance. He comments: "Directors, however, can design more efficient compensation packages that include equity-based compensation. Contracts that link executives' compensation to the outcome of their actions reduce the effort and expertise required of directors for effective oversight" (1995, 180). One implication is that the advantage of outside directors derives not from their providing more effective monitoring but from their installing incentive arrangements that are designed to ensure that managers operate in the best interests of shareholders.

23 Interestingly, Magnan, St-Onge, and Thorne (1995) find that the association between size and compensation is *stronger* for Canadian than for US firms, but Elitzur and Halpern (1995) find the opposite. The latter present evidence suggesting that the source of the relationship is salaries, rather than bonuses.

tion in the natural resources sector), cross-country comparisons should ideally take this variation into account.

- The presence of a poison pill may blunt the effectiveness of the corporate control market, facilitating managerial pay excesses.[24]
- The presence of a dual-class capital structure may affect compensation. Elitzur and Halpern (1995), for example, find that the presence of a dual-class structure has a positive effect on executive salaries (but not on bonuses). The effect is stronger in widely held than in controlled firms.
- At least in the United States, "golden parachutes" have become a common feature of executive pay packages (see Lambert and Larker, 1985).[25] To the extent that golden parachutes are less common in other countries, the difference affects total pay packages and may skew cross-country comparisons. It should be noted, however, that US evidence (ibid.) suggests that golden parachutes align managerial and shareholder interests in the case of a hostile takeover. Because the cost may outweigh the benefit, simply adding the prospective cost of managerial golden parachutes to other aspects of pay to determine total compensation may be misleading.
- The reporting of executive compensation is sensitive to the characteristics of the sample (such as average firm size) and to the varieties of compensation examined. Some studies calculate only salaries and bonuses; others add to this stock options and other forms of incentive compensation. Yet others add to this mixture stock ownership and other factors affecting executive remuneration.[26] Further, there appear to be important differ-

24 Elitzur and Halpern (1995) find some evidence that the presence of a poison pill results in higher executive compensation (through their impact on bonuses). Curiously, however, the evidence is stronger in relation to companies with a 15 percent or greater share block than for widely held companies, for which one would expect the greatest impact.

25 A golden parachute provides compensation to executives when there is a change in the control of the firm.

26 The study by Abowd and Bognanno (1995), for example, examines base salary, bonus, long-term incentive pay (such as stock options), and the value of perquisites. It also adjusts for taxation and public benefits receivable by executives.

ences in the manner in which compensation is computed. *Forbes*, for example, places a value on stock options given to US executives equal to the difference between market price and strike price (see Hardy 1985), while a Canadian survey by the accounting and management consulting firm KPMG (1995) assumes that the value of options issued equals the full market price of the optioned stock.

- A variety of different performance measures are used in attempting to relate compensation to performance. Some studies use accounting-based variables, such as return on assets; others use stock performance. Accounting- and stock-based performance measures frequently paint quite different pictures of the relationship between executive compensation and performance (see, for example, Magnan, St-Onge, and Thorne 1995).
- Managerial risk aversion may differ from one country to another. For example, it is often suggested (although, regrettably, without empirical support) that Canadians are more risk averse than Americans. If that perception is true, the optimal pay package in Canada should have a lower pay/performance sensitivity than in the United States.[27]
- Executive compensation is likely to be insensitive to short-term exchange rate movements. Because exchange rates fluctuate randomly, this insensitivity introduces an element of random fluctuation from year to year into both cardinal and ordinal rankings of executive compensation in different countries.
- Firms that are interlisted may compensate their executives differently from those that are not. Elitzur and Halpern (1995) find evidence of this phenomenon for Canadian firms.[28]

27 Interestingly, Magnan, St-Onge, and Thorne (1995) find a *stronger* pay/performance sensitivity in widely held Canadian companies than in US companies. This study fails to include the value of stock options, however.

28 Examining Canadian firms, the authors find that closely held (but not widely held) interlisted firms pay higher salaries than noninterlisted firms. They suggest that the reason may be a higher opportunity cost for executives of interlisted firms and/or the greater skills required to manage an interlisted company. There is also evidence that interlisted firms are priced in an international market, while noninterlisted firms are priced in the domestic market (see Mittoo 1992).

- Because of cultural or other factors, executives in different countries may tend to differ in age. The median age of presidents of large Japanese firms, for example, is seven years greater than that of presidents of large US firms (Kaplan 1994, 517 and 521). As discussed briefly below, executive age is a factor that may influence the design of an efficient compensation package.
- Private benefits from employment and public benefits financed from tax dollars can be regarded as substitutes. An executive considering moving from one country to another considers not only the employer-provided private benefits but also the government-provided benefits. Thus, an effective comparison of executive compensation in different countries must involve not merely a comparison of after-tax private benefits but of publicly provided benefits as well.[29]

Canada on the International Stage

Now that the Ontario Securities Commission requires disclosure of executive salaries for publicly traded firms, cross-country comparisons that include Canada are possible. For example, *Forbes* reports that the median salary plus bonus for CEOs of large US firms was $993,000 in 1994 (Hardy 1995); a survey by KPMG (1995) finds that in the same year the median pay for Canadian CEOs of large companies was $494,000. Using 1993 figures (which yielded a similar ratio) and a study by Towers Perrin, *Canadian Business* states:

> Canadian chief executives are a world-class bargain. In a survey of 19 major countries by compensation specialists Towers Perrin, Canadian CEOs ranked 11th in average compensation. They lagged far behind their US counterparts, and fell short by smaller margins to chief executives in such countries as Argentina, Japan, France and Switzerland. (Crawford 1994, 17.)[30]

---

29 Such an analysis sounds like a tall order, but one study, by Abowd and Bognanno (1995), does precisely this; I discuss it below.

30 There do appear to be a few Canadian outliers. Frank Stronach of Magna International easily tops the all-time pay list at $47 million for fiscal year 1994/95...

How meaningful are these raw comparisons? Perhaps not very, for the reasons outlined above. Before any truly useful comparisons can be made, Canadian and foreign compensation must be adjusted for the size of the firms in the respective samples, performance (that of Canadian firms has significantly lagged that of US firms in the past ten years or more — see Magnan, St-Onge, and Thorne 1995), the industry of sample firms (Canadian public firms are highly concentrated in the natural resources sector), the presence of controlling and institutional shareholders, tax burden, and so on. In addition, all aspects of compensation (including benefits flowing from stock ownership), not merely salary plus bonus, need to be compared. Ideally, adjustments should be made for the comparative probabilities of dismissal for poor performance (as is done in the Jensen and Murphy [1990b] study of US compensation).

A study by Abowd and Bognanno (1995) adjusts for some (but not all) of these factors. It examines all elements of compensation, including base salary and bonus, long-term compensation, and the value of all benefits and perquisites for 12 countries — Canada, the United States, and ten countries of the Organisation for Economic Co-operation and Development (OECD) over the 1984–92 period.

Before adjusting for taxes and public benefits, Abowd and Bognanno's study offers support to *Canadian Business*'s view that Canadian executives are a "world-class bargain." Canadian CEOs ranked tenth in terms of total real compensation; only CEOs in Sweden and the Netherlands earned less. By contrast, the total compensation paid to CEOs in the United States was significantly higher than in any other jurisdiction.

Between 1984 and 1992, real CEO pay increased in every jurisdiction that Abowd and Bognanno studied. Indeed, in most jurisdictions

Note 30 - cont'd.

...(Van Alphen 1995, B1). He also posted the second highest pay in 1993/94, at $41 million, followed by Peter Munk's $32 million in 1991 as chairman of Barrick Gold Corp. (Mathias 1995, 10). As in the United States, these large pay packages derived most of their value from the exercise of stock options and reflected extremely good corporate performance. Most other reported salaries seem modest by comparison with US salaries.

(not just the United States), the increases were spectacular — often more than 100 percent. In Canada, the increase was modest compared with that in most jurisdictions.[31]

When Abowd and Bognanno adjust for taxes, purchasing power, and the value of public benefits, however, a rather different picture emerges. Canadian CEOs stand third in the compensation sweepstakes, behind only British and US CEOs. Moreover, the increase in real pay for Canadian CEOs between 1988 and 1992 puts them approximately in the middle of the pack (ibid., 79).[32]

In general, most of the evidence concerning executive compensation comes from the United States, and most of these studies focus on firms that are both widely held and very large by Canadian standards. For this and the other reasons noted, Canadian policymakers should be very cautious about assuming that the US evidence applies wholesale to the Canadian market.

Magnan, St-Onge, and Thorne emphasize this point. They find:

> [T]here are four statistically significant differences between the strength and/or the direction of the determinants of executive compensation between Canada and the U.S.: 1) executive compensation is less responsive to firm size in U.S. firms than in Canadian firms; 2) executive compensation is more responsive to return on equity in U.S. firms than in Canadian firms; 3) the influence of ownership structure on the association between firm performance and executive compensation is greater in U.S. than in Canadian firms; and 4) a significant association between stock market performance and executive compensation is generally found only in widely-held firms in Canada and in closely-held firms in the U.S. (1995, 305).[33]

31 Unfortunately, Abowd and Bognanno lack data for 1984. However, Canada ranked ninth in the increase in CEO compensation between 1988 and 1992 (ibid., 71).

32 Interestingly, Canadian manufacturing employees stood eighth in the list of unadjusted compensation but topped it when after-tax compensation and public benefits were combined (ibid., 73 and 79). Because Canadian CEOs were lower in both lists, they appear to be more of a bargain than Canadian workers.

33 But compare Elitzur and Halpern (1995), whose results, described above, are not entirely consistent with those of Magnan, St-Onge, and Thorne.

The Past Ten Years

The evidence of Jensen and Murphy (1990b) is that, in the United States, real CEO compensation for the largest firms fell slightly from the 1930s to the 1980s, despite a great increase in the average size of the corporations in the sample (and the fact that size is strongly correlated with pay, both cross-sectionally and longitudinally). The authors also find a much closer association between pay and performance in the 1930s than in the 1980s. Much of the pay/performance relationship in the 1930s was derived from CEO stock ownership, rather than the award of bonuses or stock options.

Jensen and Murphy's evidence also shows, however, that real CEO salaries increased quite significantly from the 1970s to the 1980s.[34] Moreover, in the past ten years, executive salaries appear to have experienced further large run-ups, mostly as a result of the new-found popularity of stock option programs ("Nice Work," *The Economist*, December 10, 1994). *Forbes* indicates, for example, that "in 1993...80% of the compensation of our top 25 corporate chiefs came from exercising stock options. That figure was also 80% in 1992" (Hardy 1994)[35]

Michael Eisner's astonishing $203 million compensation in 1993 derived mostly from the exercise of stock options. It should be noted, however, that this bounty did not reflect his performance in

34 The published paper was preceded by a working paper (Jensen and Murphy 1988) that indicates CEO compensation in 1986 dollars averaged $813,000 in salary and bonus between 1934 and 1938, but only $645,000 between 1974 and 1986. The final study focuses on a shorter period in the mid-1980s and finds near equivalence of 1930s' and 1980s' salaries in real dollars.

35 More generally, *Forbes* reports that, for 1994, the median salary and bonus in its sample (which closely corresponds to the Jensen and Murphy sample) [1988; 1990b] was $993,000 in 1994 dollars, which was 11 percent higher than in 1993 The value of stock options exercised increased median pay to $1.3 million. Thus, stock options represented about 24 percent of total compensation for the firms in the *Forbes* sample (Hardy 1995). By contrast, Jensen and Murphy (1990b), whose data sample also includes large companies but terminates in the mid-1980s, find that stock options represented only about 8 percent of total compensation. Abowd and Bognanno (1995) find that the increases in compensation are indeed attributable to the proliferation of stock options.

1993 alone; rather, it derived from the cashing in of options realized over approximately ten years at the helm of Disney, during which the company's share price rose more than sixfold (Hardy 1994). In fact, during the *five* years ending in 1993, Eisner's total compensation was $237 million. His total pay for 1994 was about one-tenth his total pay in 1993, and the highest total compensation of any CEO in 1994 was $29 million (Hardy 1995).

It is tempting to observe that the people who complain the loudest about executive compensation are often those who advocate a greater relationship between pay and performance. It does not seem untoward to suggest that, if this is what they truly want, then they should live with the consequences of this relationship (that is, high pay in good years).

Because of wealth constraints and the size of public corporations, most executives today are unable to own the same fraction of large public corporations that executives did in the 1930s. Stock options are thus an alternative means for creating an incentive to perform.[36]

Comparisons with Other Organizational Forms

Despite all the hoopla about the pay of corporate executives, little attention has been focused on the fact that for many years the salaries of the top 100 Wall Street financiers have tended to make corporate executives look like slum dwellers. In 1987, when most corporate executives were looking longingly upward at the $10 million mark, Michel David-Weill, head of the investment banking firm of Lazard Frères, made $125 million (Price et al. 1987, 30). In 1988, the winner of the compensation sweepstakes was Michael Milken, whose junk

36 Indeed, the exercise of these options enhances the executive's stock ownership, again increasing his or her incentives. Unfortunately, many executives promptly sell shares acquired under options, leading some policymakers to advocate the issuance of "restricted" shares (shares that cannot be sold for some period of time, such as five years, after exercise of the options). Such plans are not observed in Canada, perhaps because they are not tax effective. (See Elitzur and Halpern 1995.)

bond activities netted him almost $200 million[37] (Taub et al. 1989). George Soros, however, is the all-time winner, surpassing even his list-topping remunerations of $117 million in 1991 and $650 million in 1992 with a whopping $1.1 billion in 1993 (see Taub and Carey 1992, 36; Taub, Byrnes, and Carey 1993, 35; Taub and Carey 1994, 30).

In general, the yearly lists of the top 100 earners on Wall Street are dominated by hedge fund managers[38] such as Soros. In addition to fee income earned on assets under administration — 1 percent, for example, for George Soros — hedge fund managers earn incentive compensation that ranges from 15 percent to 33 percent of the fund's capital appreciation — 15 percent for Soros, although more typically 20 percent (Taub and Carey 1992, 36). US venture capital fund managers receive similar remuneration. Fee income averages about 2½ percent of assets, and the managers typically keep 20 percent of the fund's capital appreciation (Sahlman 1990). Although the performance of venture funds has not been as striking as that of hedge funds, it appears to be commensurate with their risk (ibid.).

Comparing the remuneration of hedge and venture fund managers with that of corporate managers presents some dangers. Hedge and venture fund teams are typically much smaller than a corporate management team, so the decisions of these managers have a more instrumental impact on the performance of the organization (ibid.). The recent emergence[39] and startling success of these organizational forms, however, supply interesting evidence on the efficacy of pay for performance remuneration.[40]

---

37 Somewhat tarnished, perhaps, by a subsequent jail sentence for insider trading and other securities law violations.

38 A hedge fund is essentially a risky mutual fund for institutional investors and wealthy individuals, in which the managers have carte blanche to invest not only in stocks and bonds but currencies, derivatives (such as indexes and futures), commodities, real estate, and so on.

39 Venture funds date from 1946, but they did not command significant assets until the 1980s (see Bygrave and Timmons 1992, ch. 2). Hedge funds first appeared in the 1980s.

40 Jensen and Murphy (1990b) discuss franchise and leveraged buyout partnerships as other examples of high pay/performance relationships that have been enormously successful.

The Danger of the Procrustean Bed

In judging the propriety of individual compensation schemes, both market players and regulators should bear in mind that optimal compensation arrangements are likely to vary considerably across different types of firms.[41] Factors that are important include the following:

Firm Size. Because of the comparative absence of market oversight that results from having fewer institutional investors and analysts following the stock of small firms (see Daniels and MacIntosh 1991; MacIntosh 1994b), the importance of pay for performance may be greater for such firms. There is evidence that this is the case,[42] especially for very small firms.

Industry. The potential value executives add to the enterprise is likely to vary from one industry to another. For example, the executives of a highly regulated utility can likely add less value than executives of a freshly floated high-technology concern, for which the number of strategic choices and the potential capital appreciation are far greater.[43] Empirically, compensation practices vary from one industry to another, in both the United States and Canada (Gerhart and Milkovich 1990; Elitzur and Halpern 1995; KPMG 1995). And indeed, in small, high-tech firms (especially in the early stages of develop-

41 The view that optimal compensation arrangements tend to be firm specific has empirical support. For example, Brickley, Bhagat, and Lease (1985) find that a heterogeneous variety of changes to long-range compensation arrangements cause share prices to rise. They conclude that different types of firms may have different optimal compensation arrangements. Other support for this view is canvassed in this section.

42 Compare "The Buck Stopped Here" (*Forbes*, November 7, 1994, p. 258), which lists the best-paid small-firm executives and the relative proportions of different types of pay, with Hardy (1995), which contains the same information for large firms.

43 Lambert, Larcker, and Weigelt suggest "[d]ifferences in competition across input and output markets and variation in production technology should lead to differences in the structure of compensation across industries" (1993, 450).

ment), managers typically earn small salaries and take a large fraction of their compensation in incentive pay (Sahlman 1990).[44] Managerial risk aversion may also vary from one industry to another. The managers of small, high-tech concerns are likely, for example, to be less risk averse than the managers of public utilities.

Cash Flow and Earnings Variability. Some firms are cash cows: firms with a steady and reliable cash flow. Others are question marks: high-growth firms with unreliable cash flow. Given differences in upside potential, stock options are likely to be a more potent motivator for question marks than for cash cows. Moreover, given the uncertain cash flow of question marks, the payment of noncash compensation clearly benefits the firm by reducing its total fixed charges (and hence the probability of bankruptcy). For this reason, one would expect to see question marks pay less cash compensation than cash cows. A countervailing factor arises, however, from the fact that executive pay schemes reflect a tradeoff between incentive and insurance (or risk-sharing) elements. In firms with more variable cash flow, the insurance element is likely to be more important to the executive. Thus, in general, one might expect that the more variable the firm's earnings, the higher the fixed component of pay. Garen (1994) offers evidence that this is the case. To the extent that question marks have more variable earnings, this operates as an offset to the desirability of using incentive compensation for such firms.

Executive Age. As Iacobucci notes, horizon problems need to be taken into account when designing a compensation package. In particular, as an executive nears retirement, his horizon is likely to diverge more and more from that of the firm, possibly biasing investment and financing decisions, reducing the incentive to work hard, and raising the likelihood of other agency costs. (As Fama [1980] might put it, the likelihood of a full "ex post settling up" declines as retirement

44 See also the letters to the editor in *Harvard Business Review*, January-February 1994, pp. 29–32.

looms.[45]) Thus, an optimal compensation package for older executives may look different from one for younger executives (see Smith and Watts 1989).

If tournament theories explain executive compensation, then it is not so much age that one worries about as the absence of tournament incentives for chief executives at the top of the hierarchy. Once the executive wins the tournament and reaches the top, the tournament is over for her (unless she hopes to compete in a further tournament external to the firm by seeking a better-paying job elsewhere). At this point, tournament theory exhausts itself, and some other theory of compensation must be used both to describe why CEOs are paid the way they are (for example, why prefer a package with stock options to one without?) and to instruct corporations how to motivate CEOs (see, generally, Lambert, Larcker, and Weigelt 1993).

The Number of Vertical Layers in the Organization. If tournament theory is correct, then pay differentials must be maintained between horizontal layers in the organization. Indeed, if executives are risk averse, tournament theory demands that pay differentials become progressively larger as one approaches the top of the hierarchy.[46] One likely result is more upward pressure on pay at the top in large organizations with many organizational layers than in smaller organizations with fewer layers. This may indeed be a partial explanation for why large firms compensate executives better than small firms.[47]

45 See also Jensen and Murphy (1990b), who find that, as executives near retirement, the probability of removal for poor performance becomes negligible.

46 Tournament theory suggests ever-larger gaps between seniority levels toward the top of the hierarchy. Lambert, Larcker, and Weigelt (1993) present evidence that this is actually the case. Indeed, using the coefficient of determination from various regression runs, tournament theory offered the best explanation of management compensation for the 303 large publicly traded firms in their sample. (See also Leonard 1990.)

47 Two other explanations are that the marginal product of executives is larger in large firms and that more executive skill is required to lead a large organization. These two explanations are perhaps alternative ways of stating the same thing. (See, generally, Rosen 1982.)

The Uncertain Benefits of Compensation Disclosure

Ontario regulators have recently moved to require greater disclosure of executive compensation arrangements. Is this a good thing?

It seems difficult to imagine that disclosure, in itself, could be harmful. There are, however, at least three theories of harm. The first (of which the second and third are perhaps special cases) is that the regulation creates costs of compliance and yields either no benefits[48] or benefits insufficient to justify its cost. The second, presented by Jensen and Murphy (1990b), is the "implicit regulation" theory, which is regularly given added credence by often unthinking diatribes in the popular press against the excesses of executive compensation (see, for example, Best 1994).

The third theory of harm, briefly touched on by Iacobucci, is that mandatory disclosure leads to a "keeping up with the Joneses" mentality among corporate executives. Those at the low end of the pay scale lobby their boards to increase their compensation.[49] In an article in *Canadian Business*, Patricia Best (1994) indicates that this has already happened at a number of Canadian corporations. Indeed, a KPMG survey of Canadian compensation shows a 22 percent increase in median salary and bonus from 1993 to 1994. Although some of the increase may have been performance related, the survey finds that,

> [w]hile high-performing companies [those beating the TSE index by 10 percent or more over five years] had a median increase in annual incentives of 55%, low-performing companies [those whose performance trailed the TSE index by 10% or more over 5 years] paid out annual incentives 37% higher in 1994. (1995, 19.)

48 Or indeed negative benefits, as under the Jensen and Murphy (1990) theory of implicit regulation.

49 This theory is obviously inconsistent with the implicit regulation theory, in which mandated disclosure leads to compensation that is *lower* than the optimal amount (in addition to embodying too little pay/performance sensitivity).

Further, from 1993 to 1994, there was a 9 percent increase in median base salary alone.

This evidence seems consistent with a keeping up with the Joneses mentality. Mandatory disclosure of shareholder salaries may, therefore, have resulted in Canadian shareholders' being worse off.

Shareholders and Executive Compensation

Policymakers have a twofold task. They must decide not only whether to intervene in markets to correct market failures but also whether to intervene with disclosure regulation or more intrusive merit regulation, such as mandating the use of independent compensation committees. Regulating at a level higher than that at present would seem to be a mistake. As Iacobucci properly emphasizes and as I have been at pains to point out in this comment, determining optimal executive compensation is a highly complicated matter. Many factors are likely to influence a particular board of directors' selection of a pay package. Even in the United States, where the empirical record is highly developed, it is difficult to identify with great confidence particular cases of excessive remuneration.

Although the market may not remedy every excess, it is likely to remedy excesses more cost effectively than heavy-handed regulation. Where once compensation excesses may have gone unnoticed, institutional shareholders increasingly are turning their attention to this issue. Indeed, in the past few years, after decades of dormancy, institutional investors appear finally to have found their voice. In the United States, a spate of powerful CEOs of large public corporations — including Anthony D'Amato of Borden, John Akers of IBM, Kay Whitmore of Eastman Kodak, John Sculley of Apple Computer, Paul Lego of Westinghouse Electric, James Robinson III of American Express, and Robert Stempel of General Motors — have been removed at the behest of institutional shareholders.

In addition, following changes to US Securities and Exchange Commission regulations permitting shareholder proposals on compensation matters,[50] *Forbes* reports that by mid-1995 shareholders had already made 40 proposals to reduce *directors'* pensions,[51] and a proposal to eliminate directors' pensions at B.F. Goodrich received 49 percent of the vote (Linden and Lenzner 1995). Shareholder proposals dealing with executive pay have also become more common in the United States (Brownstein and Panner 1992). More generally, the focus of shareholder proposals in that country has shifted from socially oriented to governance oriented, and the number of the latter has increased dramatically (Linden and Rotenier 1994).

Such proposals are often brought by institutional, rather than retail, shareholders. Indeed, James Heard, president of Institutional Shareholder Services, a major activist on behalf of US institutional investors, states: "executive compensation has become a major concern of institutional investors" (1995, 749). He argues that, in contrast to the popular press, US institutions have focused their efforts on *how* executives are paid, rather than *how much*.[52]

Traditionally, Canadian institutional investors have tended to be active only behind closed doors. Yet the number of Canadian cases in which institutions have gone public with opposition to particular management initiatives has increased at an extraordinary rate over the past five years (MacIntosh 1996). A recent dust-up over Northern Telecom's share option plan indicates that institutional owners will not be shy about taking on management when they think that a compensation plan is excessive (Chianello 1995; Mackenzie 1995).[53]

Another indication that bad performers tend to be routed out by either internal or external market forces is the popularity among

---

50 As described in Iacobucci. See also Salwen (1992).

51 The practice of paying pensions to directors appears to be a relatively recent innovation.

52 Heard (1995) reviews institutional shareholder activism in the United States in relation to compensation plans.

53 The institutional opposition resulted in a scaling back of Northern Telecom's proposed option plan. That battle is only one of a number of cases in which institutional investors have raised concerns about corporate share option plans (see MacIntosh 1996).

institutional investors of "clunker" (or "contrarian") investing — buying underperforming duds.[54] The assumption that frequently motivates such investment behavior is that sooner or later the managers who are responsible for poor performance will be replaced. For example, a report on Robert Monks, a successful clunker investor and a former institutional investor activist, states:

> Excessive executive compensation is often a plus. Has management received salary increases as the stock has sunk? That contributed to the demise of Anthony D'Amato at Borden, a Monks holding. Monks thinks the stock, recently at $13, could climb to $20 if the new broom sweeps clean. (Berss 1994, 189.)

The new-found power of institutional investors adds to the argument that there is little need for additional regulation (although, as I argued earlier, the entire market context is important, including the efficacy of takeover markets and so on).

Relative Pay

Holmstrom (1979) demonstrates that any information that helps distinguish the agent's effort from background noise is valuable in setting the compensation contract. In other words, a manager's pay should be influenced only by those things over which that manager has control. External events, such as market movements, or even internal events unconnected with executive effort or skill should be factored out of the compensation package.

Antle and Smith (1986) find evidence suggesting that, at least in some cases, US compensation packages are crafted to do this. It seems clear, however, that pay packages at many companies make little or no attempt to wash out factors over which executives have no control. Murphy (1985), for example, finds the overall stock index more useful than stock performance *relative* to the market in explain-

54 Many institutional investors engage in such trading strategies (see MacIntosh and Schwartz 1995).

ing total executive compensation.[55] Garen (1994) also finds little evidence of the use of relative pay schemes.

It also seems clear that making pay more sensitive to relative performance would not be difficult. Antle and Smith (1986) indicate that relative performance data is readily available, and Nalbantian (1993) shows how pay packages can be crafted to take relative performance into account. In my view, paying for relative performance is likely to become a new mantra of executive compensation gurus in years to come.[56]

Changing the Strike Price of Options

The issue of pay for relative performance is connected with that of boards of directors' reducing the strike price of executive options when the firm's stock market price goes down. Crystal (1991) criticizes this practice, but Iacobucci argues that it may not be inappropriate in order to avoid excessive risk taking by managers whose only chance of cashing in on the options is to dramatically increase firm performance. There is an additional reason for recasting the strike price: poor stock market performance may have nothing to do with executive performance. Although lowering the strike price *may* reward bad managers, it may also be a way of partially washing market-wide factors out of executive compensation. Clearly, however, better tools (such as relative compensation, discussed above) are available.

55 Like Antle and Smith (1986), however, Murphy also finds evidence consistent with the view that some companies make an attempt to wash extraneous factors out of executive compensation. Thus, in his sample, Murphy finds relative performance a better predictor of bonuses than unadjusted corporate performance (1985, 40).

56 Daniels and Morck (1995) also stress the importance of relative pay. See also Gibbons and Murphy (1990). Murphy (1995) argues strenuously in favor of retaining stock-based compensation arrangements and presents guidance that options and restricted stock account for more than three-quarters of all CEO compensation. He does not, however, exclude the possibility of relative pay schemes (ibid., 724).

Phantom Options and Stock Appreciation Rights

Iacobucci does not address the relationship between management share ownership and firm value. Some evidence, however, suggests that firm value may actually decline with increasing management ownership (over some ranges) because of greater management entrenchment. Clearly, this problem is likely to occur only for widely held corporations. One way to avoid entrenchment in such corporations is to compensate executives using phantom stock (or stock appreciation rights), which do not result in the issuance of shares.[57]

A countervailing consideration, however, is that the greatest part of the pay/performance sensitivity in CEO compensation packages (at least until the mid-1980s) has come from share ownership.

Clearly, we need more investigation of the relationships among management pay, compensation, and firm performance (see, generally, Lambert, Larcker, and Weigelt 1993).

Outside Directors and Stock Options

The idea of remunerating outside directors solely in stock options, in order to generate appropriate performance incentives, has recently drawn much discussion (see, for example, Daniels and Morck 1995; Mackenzie 1995; Linden and Lenzner 1995). In fact, some companies have already adopted such plans (Linden and Lenzner 1995). It is doubtful that such plans are appropriate for all companies. Risk-averse outside directors may not be willing to accept their entire compensation in the form of options. Such payment may give them an incentive to take on excessively risky projects. Moreover, many plans are designed so that options vest only over a period of years, in order to ensure long-term service. Such plans increase outside directors' dependence on the goodwill of the CEO since they will not

57 Many executives, however, sell the shares they derive from stock options, alleviating concerns about entrenchment (see Mathias 1995).

realize benefits without prolonged service and it is typically the CEO who determines yearly nominations for directorships.[58]

Empirically, the case in favor of options for directors is shaky. In a sample of very large US firms, Morck, Shleifer, and Vishny (1988) find a positive relationship between outside directors' holdings and firm value. Yet most outside directors (save those placed on boards as a result of proxy contests) do not have holdings sufficiently large to serve as a potent motivator. Mehran (1995) suggests that most stock option plans will fail to create appropriate incentives; in his sample of comparatively small firms, he finds no significant relationship between outside directors' equity and firm performance.

Putting Executive Pay into Perspective

Repeated bashing of executive pay in the popular press has created the impression that excessive pay results in vastly diminished returns for shareholders. Consider the following, however. Murphy (1995, 726) calculates that, in 1992, the total compensation paid to the CEOs of the 1,000 largest US firms was $2.2 billion; however, the total market capitalization of these firms was $3.4 trillion. If every CEO had worked for free in 1992, shareholder returns for that year, which averaged 24 percent, would have increased by only 0.06 percentage points.

These extraordinary figures do not suggest that designing effective compensation packages is unimportant: properly motivating executives is of vital importance to ensuring continued wealth creation in the economy. They do, however, support the claim of Jensen and Murphy (1990a) that the executive compensation debate should focus not on *how much* executives are paid, but on *how* they are paid.

58 Indeed, the Cadbury Report of the London Stock Exchange counsels against the adoption of director option plans because of their potential effect on director independence. The practice of leaving director nominations in the hands of CEOs is changing, however; it is not recommended by either the Cadbury Report or the report of the Toronto Stock Exchange Committee on Corporate Governance (1994).

References

Abowd, John M., and Michael L. Bognanno. 1995. "International Differences in Executive and Managerial Compensation." In Richard B. Freeman and Lawrence F. Katz, eds., *Differences in Wage Structures*. Chicago: University of Chicago Press.

Alchian, Armen A., and Harold Demsetz. 1972. "Production, Information Costs, and Economic Organization." *American Economic Review* 62 (4): 722–795.

Antle, Rick, and Abbie Smith. 1986. "An Empirical Investigation of the Relative Performance Evaluation of Corporate Executives." *Journal of Accounting Research* 24 (1): 1–39.

Baker, George P. 1988. "Compensation and Incentives: Practice vs. Theory." *Journal of Finance* 43 (3): 593–616.

Benston, George J. 1985. "The Self-Serving Management Hypothesis: Some Evidence." *Journal of Accounting and Economics* 7 (1–3): 67–84.

Berss, Marcia. 1994. "Clunker Investing." *Forbes*, June 20, p. 181.

Best, Patricia. 1994. "Are You Worth $1 Million a Year?" *Canadian Business*, July, p. 28.

Bhagat, Sanjai, James A. Brickley, and Ronald C. Lease. 1985. "Incentive Effects of Stock Purchase Plans." *Journal of Financial Economics* 14 (2): 195–215.

Brickley, James A., Sanjai Bhagat, and Ronald C. Lease. 1985. "The Impact of Long-Range Compensation Plans on Shareholder Wealth." *Journal of Accounting and Economics* 7 (1–3): 115–129.

Brownstein, Andrew R., and Morris J. Panner. 1992. "Who Should Set CEO Pay? The Press? Congress? Shareholders?" *Harvard Business Review*, May-June, pp. 28–38.

Bygrave, William D., and Jeffrey A. Timmons. 1992. *Venture Capital at the Crossroads*. Boston: Harvard Business School Press.

Chianello, Joanne. 1995. "Investors Battle NorTel." *Financial Post*, April 18, p. 1.

Coffee, John C. 1986. "Shareholders versus Managers: The Strain in the Corporate Web." *Michigan Law Review* 85 (1): 1–109.

Coughlan, Anne T., and Ronald M. Schmidt. 1985. "Executive Compensation, Management Turnover, and Firm Performance: An Empirical Investigation." *Journal of Accounting and Economics* 7 (1–3): 43–66.

Crawford, Michael. 1994. "Peanuts for Elephants." *Canadian Business*, July, p. 16.

Crystal, G. 1991. *In Search of Excess: The Overcompensation of American Executives*. New York: W.W. Norton.

Daniels, Ronald J., and Jeffrey G. MacIntosh. 1991. "Toward a Distinctive Canadian Corporate Law Regime." *Osgoode Hall Law Journal* 29 (4): 863–933.

———, and Randall Morck. 1995. "Canadian Corporate Governance: Policy Options." In Ronald J. Daniels and Randall Morck, eds., *Corporate Decision Making in Canada*. Calgary: University of Calgary Press.

Easterbrook, Frank H. 1984. "Two Agency Cost Explanations of Dividends." *American Economic Review* 74 (4): 650–659.

Elitzur, Ramy, and Paul Halpern. 1995. "Executive Compensation and Firm Value." In Ronald J. Daniels and Randall Morck, eds., *Corporate Decision Making in Canada*. Calgary: University of Calgary Press.

Fama, Eugene F. 1980. "Agency Problems and the Theory of the Firm." *Journal of Political Economy* 88 (2): 288–367.

Finkelstein, Sydney, and Donald C. Hambrick. 1988. "Chief Executive Compensation: A Synthesis and Reconciliation." *Strategic Management Journal* 9 (6): 543–558.

Garen, John E. 1994. "Executive Compensation and Principal-Agent Theory." *Journal of Political Economy* 102 (6): 1175–1199.

Gerhart, Barry, and George T. Milkovich. 1990. "Organizational Differences in Managerial Compensation and Financial Performance." *Academy of Management Journal* 33 (4): 663–691.

Gibbons, Robert, and Kevin J. Murphy. 1990. "Relative Performance Evaluation for Chief Executive Officers." *Industrial and Labor Relations Review* 43 (February, special issue): 30-S–51-S.

Hardy, Eric S. 1994. "Marathon Men." *Forbes*, May 23, p. 140.

———. 1995. "Payday for America's 800 Top Chief Executives." *Forbes*, May 22, p. 184.

Haubrich, Joseph G. 1994. "Risk Aversion, Performance Pay, and the Principal-Agent Problem." *Journal of Political Economy* 102 (2): 258–276.

Healy, Patricia. 1985. "The Effect of Bonus Schemes on Accounting Decisions." *Journal of Accounting and Economics* 7 (1–3): 85–108.

Heard, James E. 1995. "Executive Compensation: Perspective of the Institutional Investors." *University of Cincinnati Law Review* 63 (2): 749–767.

Holmstrom, Bengt. 1979. "Moral Hazard and Observability." *Rand Journal of Economics* 10 (spring): 74–91.

Jensen, Michael C. 1986. "Agency Costs of Free Cash Flow, Corporate Finance, and Takeovers." *American Economic Review* 76 (2): 323–329.

———, and William Meckling. 1976. "Theory of the Firm: Managerial Behavior, Agency Costs, and Ownership Structure." *Journal of Financial Economics* 3 (3): 305–360.

———, and Kevin J. Murphy. 1988. "Performance Pay and Top Management Incentives." Harvard Business School Working Paper 88-059. Cambridge, Mass., Harvard University.

———, and Kevin J. Murphy. 1990a. "CEO Incentives — It's Not How Much You Pay, but How." *Harvard Business Review*, May-June, pp. 138–149.

———, and Kevin J. Murphy. 1990b. "Performance Pay and Top Management Incentives." *Journal of Political Economy* 98 (2): 225–264.

Kaplan, Steven N. 1994. "Top Executive Rewards and Firm Performance: A Comparison of Japan and the United States." *Journal of Political Economy* 102 (3): 510–546.

Kostiuk, Peter F. 1990. "Firm Size and Executive Compensation." *Journal of Human Resources* 25 (1): 90–105.

KPMG. 1995. *Executive Compensation Practices in the TSE 300 Companies 1995*. Toronto.

Lambert, Richard A., and David F. Larcker. 1985. "Golden Parachutes, Executive Decision-Making, and Shareholder Wealth." *Journal of Accounting and Economics* 7 (1–3): 179–204.

———, David F. Larcker, and Keith Weigelt. 1993. "The Structure of Organizational Incentives." *Administrative Science Quarterly* 38 (3): 438–461.

Leonard, Jonathan S. 1990. "Executive Pay and Firm Performance." *Industrial and Labor Relations Review* 43 (February, special issue): 13-S–29-S.

Linden, Dana Wechsler, and Nancy Rotenier. 1994. "Good-bye to Berle & Means." *Forbes*, January 3, p. 100.

———, and Robert Lenzner. 1995. "The Cosseted Director." *Forbes*, May 22, p. 168. With Frank Wolfe.

McConnell, J.J., and H. Servaes. 1990. "Additional Evidence on Equity Ownership and Corporate Value." *Journal of Financial Economics* 27(2): 595–612.

MacIntosh, Jeffrey G. 1994a. "Corporate Governance in Canada: A Broad-Brush Assessment." *In Securities Regulation: Issues and Perspectives*. Scarborough, Ont.: Carswell.

———. 1994b. "The Role of Institutional and Retail Shareholders in Canadian Capital Markets." *Osgoode Hall Law Journal* 32 (2): 371–472.

———. 1996. "Institutional Shareholders and Corporate Governance in Canada." *Canadian Business Law Journal* 26 (2): 145–188.

———, and Larry Schwartz. 1995. "Do Institutional and Controlling Shareholders Increase Corporate Value?" In Ronald J. Daniels and Randall Morck, eds., *Corporate Decision Making in Canada*. Calgary: University of Calgary Press.

Mackenzie, William M. 1995. "Options, Too Much of a Good Thing?" *Corporate Governance Review* 7 (3): 1–5.

Magnan, Michel L., Sylvie St-Onge, and Linda Thorne. 1995. "A Comparative Analysis of the Determinants of Executive Compensation between Canadian and US firms." *Industrial Relations—Quebec* 50: 297–317.

Mathias, Philip. 1995. "Just How Fat Are These Cats?" *Financial Post*, November 4, weekly ed., p. 10.

Mehran, Hamid. 1995. "Executive Compensation Structure, Ownership, and Firm Performance." *Journal of Financial Economics* 38 (2): 163–184.

Miller, Merton H., and Myron S. Scholes. 1982. "Executive Compensation, Taxes, and Incentives." In William Sharpe and Catherine Cootner, eds., *Financial Economics: Essays in Honor of Paul Cootner*. Englewood Cliffs, NJ: Prentice Hall.

Mittoo, Usha R. 1992. "Additional Evidence on Integration in the Canadian Stock Market." *Journal of Finance* 47 (5): 2035–2054.

Morais, Richard, Gale Eisenstodt, and Steve Kichen. 1993. "The Global Boss' Pay: Where (and How) the Money Is." *Forbes*, June 7, p. 90.

Morck, Randall, Andrei Shleifer, and Robert W. Vishny. 1988. "Management Ownership and Market Valuation." *Journal of Financial Economics* 20 (1): 293–316.

Murphy, Kevin J. 1985. "Corporate Performance and Managerial Remuneration." *Journal of Accounting and Economics* 7 (1–3): 11–42.

———. 1995. "Politics, Economics, and Executive Compensation." *Cincinnati Law Review* 63 (2): 713–748.

Nalbantian, Haig R. 1993. "Performance Indexing in Stock Option and Other Incentive Compensation Programs." *Compensation & Benefits Review* 25 (5): 25–40.

Price, Margaret, et al. 1987. "Scrutiny of the Bounty: Money Addicts — Wall Street's Superstars." *Financial World*, July 14, p. 38.

Rosen, Sherwin. 1982. "Authority, Control, and the Distribution of Earnings." *Bell Journal of Economics* 13 (2): 311–323.

Ross, Stephen A., and Randolph Westerfield. 1988. *Corporate Finance*. St. Louis: Times Mirror/Mosby College Publishing.

Sahlman, William A. 1990. "The Structure and Governance of Venture-Capital Organizations." *Journal of Financial Economics* 27 (2): 473–521.

Salwen, Kevin G. 1992. "The people's proxy: shareholder proposals on pay must be aired, SEC to tell 10 firms." *Wall Street Journal*, February 13, p. A1.

Smith, Clifford W., and Ross L. Watts. 1982. "Incentive and Tax Effects of Executive Compensation Plans." *Austin Journal of Management* 7 (2): 139–157.

Taub, Stephen, et al. 1989. "The Wall Street 100." *Financial World*, July 11, p. 32.

———, Nanette Byrnes, and David Carey. 1993. "The $650 Million Man." *Financial World*, July 6, p. 38.

———, and David Carey. 1992. "Wall Street's New Austerity." *Financial World*, July 21, p. 36.

———, and David Carey. 1994. "The Wall Street 100." *Financial World*, July 5, p. 30.

Tehranian, Hassan, and James F. Waegelein. 1985. "Market Reaction to Short-Term Executive Compensation Plan Adoption." *Journal of Accounting and Economics* 7 (1–3): 131–144.

Toronto Stock Exchange. Committee on Corporate Governance. 1994. *Where Were the Directors?* Toronto.

Van Alphen, Tony. 1995. "$47 million pay cheque for Magna's Stronach." *Toronto Star*, November 4, final ed., p. B1.

Vancil, Richard F. 1987. *Passing the Baton: Managing the Process of CEO Succession*. Boston: Harvard Business School Press.

Warner, Jerold B., Ross L. Watts, and Karen H. Wruck. 1988. "Stock Prices, Event Prediction, and Event Studies: An Examination of Top Management Changes." *Journal of Financial Economics* 20 (1–2): 461–492.

Weisbach, Michael S. 1988. "Outside Directors and CEO Turnover." *Journal of Financial Economics* 20 (1–2): 431–460.

Wruck, Karen Hopper. 1988. "Equity Ownership Concentration and Firm Value." *Journal of Financial Economics* 23 (1): 3–28.

Some Comments on the Marketplace

James C. Baillie

Edward Iacobucci's lucid analysis of economic and legal issues bearing on the compensation of senior executives in Canada is a worthwhile contribution to the literature. I am particularly glad that he did not attempt to reach firm conclusions. Too many generalized conclusions about the compensation of executives — particularly chief executive officers (CEOs) — are based on data that fall ludicrously short of supporting them.

On Iacobucci's overview, however, I have only a few comments to make.

The Market for CEOs

Although Iacobucci's title refers to "*executive* compensation," the paper deals almost entirely with CEOs. This focus is important; as the author notes (p. 20), the gap between salary levels for CEOs and those for their immediate subordinates is often substantial. To my mind, this gap has significance that is even greater than Iacobucci attributes to it.

If I have a fault to find with Iacobucci's analysis, it is that he appears to assume a relatively static dynamic between the corporation and its CEO; he seems to me not to give sufficient weight to the existence of a competitive market in CEOs.

My perception is that some of the key decisions affecting CEO compensation levels in Canada are made by human resource committees as they attempt to attract new CEOs. As the rate of turnover of CEOs increases,[1] the frequency with which such negotiations occur correspondingly increases. And human resource committees are far less prepared to take a chance with a CEO appointment than they are with more junior appointments in the senior executive ranks. A proven track record is almost essential when a substantial corporation recruits a CEO. Thus, I believe that there is a more competitive market for CEOs than for chief financial officers or chief operating officers.

An individual chosen by a human resource committee as its candidate for CEO can be in a strong bargaining position. He or she can point to the compensation disclosures made by comparable corporations and take the approach that the board should demonstrate confidence by awarding compensation in the first or second quartile. If successful, this argument has a ripple impact as the new compensation package becomes public and itself influences subsequent negotiations in other corporations. Thus, as John McNeil says (see Iacobucci, p. 51), disclosure requirements have an upward impact on compensation levels.

I do not wish to suggest, however, that this analysis supports the conclusion that CEOs are overcompensated. In my perception, the trend toward higher compensation in Canada and the United States has been accompanied by a trend toward lower job security and shorter tenure. Increasingly lean corporate structures and an intensely competitive environment magnify the importance of the rule of the CEO. A board of directors can fully support a seemingly high level of compensation if the individual produces results.

It is also noteworthy that the headlines focus on CEOs who have been successful. As Iacobucci notes, typical compensation packages for CEOs of public corporations include stock options and other equity-based arrangements. Few, if any, headlines result when options produce no benefit for the executive. I have seen some articles in the British press about executives who are undercompensated by

1 Which I believe to be happening — largely in consequence of increasing vigilance on the part of directors.

comparison with the performance of their corporations (for example, Lynn 1995), but if similar articles have appeared in Canada, I have missed them.

Outside Directors

As these remarks indicate, I think the free market is broadly operating as it should in determining levels of CEO compensation. But the legal and corporate governance environment is not perfect. Corporate governance practices are in a state of evolution. The pace of change has been accelerated in consequence of the responsibilities conferred specifically on compensation committees under the disclosure requirements adopted by the Ontario Securities Commission. In my experience, the practice of these committees' directly retaining compensation consultants, so that they are responsible to outside directors, rather than to executive management, is being used with increasing frequency.

Moreover, Iacobucci's concern that boards of directors act in accordance with the wishes of management in setting compensation is, I believe, becoming less justified as the process of evolution continues. Management rarely has this degree of control in a corporation that has a major or controlling shareholder — the situation for nearly 80 percent of Canada's public corporations. Such shareholders have a sufficient economic interest that the most dour commentator will be unlikely to suggest they are puppets of management. Even in corporations without a major shareholder, the independent directors are, in my experience, far from rubber stamps for management recommendations on management compensation packages.

In this connection, I have some difficulty reconciling Iacobucci's emphasis on the importance of careful scrutiny by outside directors with his concern over the "increasingly attractive pecuniary advantages of directorships" (p. 37). My perception is that compensation levels are approaching what is appropriate and desirable in order to pay senior executives of other corporations (who are typically chosen as independent directors) for the work they are expected to do in the brave new world of corporate governance. I would far rather see adequately compensated directors than undercompensated ones who serve only for reasons of prestige or personal friendship with the CEO.

Iacobucci examines the possibility of institutional investors' becoming actively involved in compensation decisions, supplementing or supporting the board of directors. I agree that some involvement by institutional investors is desirable, but I am skeptical that their involvement should be as great as Iacobucci seems to suggest. Some analysts assume that institutional investors operate on a longer timeframe than management or perhaps the board. In my experience, this assumption is often simply wrong. Institutional investors are themselves subject to the discipline of the competitive marketplace; they are often judged on performance over periods as short as quarter by quarter, and it mystifies me why some commentators (I do not necessarily include Iacobucci here) assume that they will judge their investee corporations on a timeframe longer than directors adopt.

Further, I am of the old school that believes fiduciary obligation means something. Certainly, the courts continue to tell us this. Institutional investors act — as they must — in their own best interest and according to their legal responsibilities, which are to those whose money they manage, not to the shareholders of investee corporations. (Only the directors of those corporations have fiduciary responsibilities to their shareholders.) Accordingly, I strongly believe that the law should continue to develop to accommodate institutional investors' expression of views but that no steps should be taken to enhance the ability of institutional investors to dictate corporate decisions. For example, I think that an expansion of the flexibility for shareholder proposals to dictate corporate action would not be desirable for corporate governance.

The Stock Exchanges and Regulation

As a lawyer, I should comment on legal issues flowing from Iacobucci's paper. Although I do not have much to say that deals specifically with points in his paper, an important underlying issue merits comment. This is the role of stock exchanges in formulating the regulatory environment. Two recent initiatives of the Toronto Stock Exchange (TSE) are particularly relevant: its decision to relax the rules governing employee stock options, and the publication of the report of its Committee on Corporate Governance in Canada (1994) — the Dey Report. The former bears directly and the latter indirectly on the topic of executive compensation.

In my view, a stock exchange should regulate the companies it lists only to a limited extent. Many commentators assume that such regulation is justified under the rubric of self-regulation, which is increasingly regarded as a good thing in our society. But the regulation of listed companies by a stock exchange is not self-regulation since they do not participate in formulating the rules (unless the exchange voluntarily includes their representatives on advisory committees or similar bodies). It is reasonable and, indeed, necessary for a stock exchange to dictate listing standards so that its marketplace is restricted to credible corporations with reasonably active trading volumes. Further, a stock exchange can and should dictate transfer procedures. Its entry into the realm of disclosure requirements so as to ensure a smoothly functioning market is also, in my view, justified.

But where a stock exchange purports to regulate its listed companies in a manner going beyond what is required for the effective functioning of the market, serious issues seem to me to arise. The TSE has a statutory monopoly on trading in equity securities in Ontario. In that respect, it is like a public utility. Telephone and hydro companies do not purport to regulate the morality or conduct of those who receive their services. Neither should the securities dealers who run stock exchanges attempt to dictate the corporate conduct of listed companies as a condition of maintaining their listings.

Nature abhors a vacuum, however, and the TSE has understandably rushed in to deal with issues that community consensus identifies as significant and that are not being adequately addressed by other regulators. Yet it seems to me that the position of the exchange and the fact that it is operating in a competitive environment is bound to affect the nature of the regulation it applies. I am not privy to the considerations that led the TSE to modify its policies on employee stock options, but it would not surprise me if one motivating factor was that a regime some listed companies perceived as unduly rigorous might lead those companies to delist and seek listing elsewhere. It would be understandable if this consideration resulted in a modification of the TSE rules. Similar constraints might apply to the extent of the exchange's practical ability to deal effectively with corporate governance.

In brief, I caution against continuing the trend toward having debate on regulatory change move away from the traditional arenas of corporate and securities law toward the stock exchanges, whose primary responsibility is to facilitate trading in equity securities.

Ontario Salary Disclosure

An interesting contrast with the issues canvassed in Iacobucci's paper is provided by Ontario's recent disclosure of remuneration in excess of $100,000 earned by employees of provincial and municipal governments and of other public sector institutions, including universities, hospitals, and any bodies that received $120,000 or more in transfer payments from the province.[2] The media response to the long lists of names has been mixed, ranging from incredulity that people would be paid so much (for example, Allemang 1996) to consternation that they are paid so little by comparison with corresponding positions in the private sector (for example, Simpson 1996).

What impact this disclosure will have is unclear. I predict that, unlike the private sector disclosure requirements Iacobucci discusses, Ontario's disclosure may well keep public sector remuneration down

2 The disclosures were made under the province's *Public Sector Salary Disclosure Act, 1996*. The list of salaries disclosed was published in the *Globe and Mail* (Toronto), April 2–5, 1996.

because the politics of envy may become operative without the countervail of upward pressure on CEO compensation.

Conclusion

Iacobucci's paper deals with an issue that is fraught with political and societal implications. My view is that public disclosure of executive compensation is desirable and healthy overall, although it has had significant consequences and has brought to the fore a debate that has opened some sores.

One consequence of the disclosure and of the debate is that the various pressures on executive compensation are operating openly. The upward pressure resulting from the competitive market in CEOs is increasingly being met by countervailing pressures exerted by independent directors and institutional investors. Thus, to my mind, the system is operating as it should. I hope the shrill voices calling for some form of direct governmental regulation of compensation in the private sector will be resisted.

References

Allemang, J. 1996. "Public salary disclosures stir some baser instincts." *Globe and Mail* (Toronto), April 5, p. A1.

Lynn, Matthew. 1995. "Do our bosses give value for money?" *Sunday Times* (London), November 5.

Simpson, J. 1996. "Corporate bosses are continuing to reward themselves handsomely." *Globe and Mail* (Toronto), April 16, p. A18.

Toronto Stock Exchange. Committee on Corporate Governance in Canada. 1995. [Dey Report]. *Where Were the Directors? Guidelines for Improved Corporate Governance in Canada*. Toronto.

Comments, Part III

If There Is a Problem and If Its Sources Can Be Identified, What Policy Responses Are Appropriate?

Holding Our Heads High

Edward J. Waitzer

Like the Ontario Securities Commission's (OSC's) new requirement for public companies to disclose executive compensation levels, Edward Iacobucci's excellent paper raises more questions than it answers. Both tend to be on much more solid ground in describing *what* corporations are deciding, rather than *how* and *why* such decisions are taken. With respect to the executive compensation disclosure requirement, this has been a significant deficiency noted by OSC staff.[1]

Considerable difficulty, both theoretical and practical, remains in aligning the interests of owners and managers through compensation schemes. Even if, as the tournament theory of compensation suggests, that alignment may not be the direct function of compensation levels, appropriate monitoring and oversight of management ultimately is essential to the corporate enterprise and public confidence therein. *Ex ante* solutions are clearly more cost effective than trying to solve problems once they have manifested themselves—and, presumably, lessened shareholder value. More work is required to stimulate effective oversight mechanisms.

Transparency and Monitoring

The first challenge is to achieve the objective of the disclosure requirements by making the boards' decisionmaking processes more transparent. Progress is apparent.

The views expressed in this comment do not necessarily represent those of the Ontario Securities Commission, other Commissioners, or the staff of the OSC.

1 The staff of the OSC has noted this discrepancy. For example, a recent staff report (OSC 1995) comments frequently on deficiencies relating to the quality of the compensation committee reports on how compensation levels are determined.

A second avenue that seems to be gaining currency is measures to create effective management monitoring based on board self-motivation. Proposals here include compensating directors with equity as well as dismantling retirement plans and other benefits unrelated to actual board service (see, for example, Linden 1995, 54), having proficiency standards and self-assessments for directors, and providing in proxy statements more extensive disclosures of director compensation (modeled on currently required executive compensation disclosures).[2] All might serve to align directors' interests more closely with those of a corporation's shareholders.

Shareholder Activism

Other dimensions to market discipline may also merit further consideration. For example, a traditionally proffered response to perceived compensation problems has been increased institutional shareholder activism (see, for example, Daniels and Waitzer 1994). Institutions have indeed assumed a more active role in corporate governance. Leaving aside the usually cited barriers to such activism, however, a mirror-image monitoring/accountability concern arises. Given the high degree of concentration and relational overlap in the community of institutional investors, surely the prospect of active compensation oversight within their own managerial structures is likely to inhibit their playing an active role with respect to executive compensation within investee corporations (except in egregious cases). As Yablon points out:

2 The London Stock Exchange recently published an amendment to its listing rules, implementing many of its recommendations of the Study Group on Directors' Remuneration (the Greenbury Committee — LSE 1995), including requirements that listed companies disclose information relating to directors' remuneration, make a statement of compliance with the best practice provisions regarding remuneration committees, and make a statement that full consideration has been given to the best practice provisions relating to remuneration policy, service contracts, and compensation. The Exchange also issued a consultative document with proposed rules relating to long-term incentive schemes, options, and pensions for directors.

> Financial institutions are run by corporate executives who may be receiving, or be interested in receiving, compensation at levels or in forms not very different from those that are under attack from the various shareholder groups. Such executives are unlikely to mount or join challenges to executive compensation plans because they may feel...that the compensation offered to their fellow executives is perfectly appropriate. (1992, 1893.)

Another approach to stimulating greater accountability on the part of institutional investors was recently proposed in *The Economist* ("Fat Cats and Their Cream," July 22, 1995, p. 19), in response to the release of the Greenbury Committee Report in the United Kingdom (LSE 1995). It suggested that executive pay be put to an annual vote of shareholders and that the votes of the biggest shareholders on this issue be disclosed.

Tax Policy

As with seemingly all aspects of our lives, tax policy imposes significant discipline on executive compensation, both on how it is structured and, perhaps more important, on compensation levels. Most notably, the double taxation of distributed corporate earnings encourages management to retain earnings. Often, this results in the pursuit of policies more rewarding to management than to shareholders. Although the threat of a hostile takeover remains, we are again faced with ineffective *ex ante* mechanisms.

Twenty years ago, in a submission to the Royal Commission on Corporate Concentration (Berman and Waitzer 1976, para. 9.3.1–2), a colleague and I suggested that all "mature" public corporations be required to regularly distribute their accumulated surplus over a five-year rolling period (that is, at least 20 percent annually). Such distributions would be tax free to the extent that they were reinvested in publicly traded equity securities (whether or not of the distributing corporation) within a defined period of time. Such a rule would provide a mechanism whereby individual investors, rather than corporate management, would be able to decide on the use of their assets. Sir Alan Walters (1995) has recently advanced a similar proposal.[3]

The Normative Issue

Most people agree that there are not yet — and perhaps will never be — single right answers for executive compensation methodology. Similarly, most would agree that practices are improving. Why, then, does the public fuss persist, given the demonstrable impact of market discipline and the remarkable and consistent capacity of the corporate form of organization to adapt and regenerate itself?

The basic issue in the compensation debate is more difficult to address than other governance concerns. With respect to the latter, the barriers to be overcome relate primarily to a universal aversion to accountability when focused on oneself, coupled with a limited knowledge base and the inertial forces that pertain to any organizational status quo.

Compensation practices, in contrast, raise questions about fundamental values. Hence, the public policy debate is often akin to ships passing in the night. Private sector leaders justifiably point to market discipline and the hazards of undue regulatory intervention. In contrast, those who put the issue into play (whether consumer advocates, politicians, or the media) tend to focus on an entirely different plane.

As the conservative social critic Irving Kristol has argued, alienation and distrust are bound to result if the distribution of power, privilege, and property "no longer seems in some profound sense expressive of the values that govern the lives of individuals" (1978, 267). The globalization of labor markets, coupled with the abatement of many of Canada's social transfers (which have tended

3 He proposes that corporations be required to issue two types of shares: "all earnings shares," which would require the corporation to pay out all of its earnings to shareholders, and "no earning shares." A minimum of 80 percent "all earnings shares" would be required, ensuring that earnings would be passed to the shareholders and recycled through the capital markets.

to mitigate against extreme income disparities) will heighten public sensitivity to these concerns. Compensation disclosure provides a basis for such normative judgments but little more. Evidence of its disciplining effect, absent other remedies, is far from conclusive.

Proactive Leadership

Regrettably, few private sector leaders feel comfortable with this level of discourse. A result is a tendency to become defensive, which, in turn, allows others to define the issues and, ultimately, scapegoat the system we represent. Without articulate and proactive corporate leadership, further regulatory intervention is likely.

As I have argued elsewhere (Waitzer 1994), the continuing challenge for the private sector is to face these and other values issues head on, rather than allowing others to define them (and thereby, to a great extent, the outcomes) by design or, worse, by default.[4] We need to be better prepared to articulate the values we believe in and to have the courage to back them up with consistent action. This will become increasingly imperative in order to retain — and, one hopes, build on — the underlying trust and social cohesion on which our market enterprise system depends.

The good news is that the system works remarkably well. Where we fall down is in embracing opportunities to broadcast its achievements and publicly acknowledge and promote the willingness and capacity for self-improvement.

4 For a recent discussion of regulation by default, see Bradsher (1995). One classic example is the imposition by the US Congress of a penalty tax on executive compensation of more than US$1 million. Another example is a recent proposal by certain US regulators to impose pay limits for "risky traders."

References

Berman, J., and E. Waitzer. 1976. "Submission to the Royal Commission on Corporate Concentration." Toronto.

Bradsher, K. 1995. "U.S. regulators draft pay limits for risky traders." *Globe and Mail* (Toronto), November 27, p. B9.

Daniels, R.W., and E.J. Waitzer. 1994. "Challenges to the Citadel: A Brief Overview of Recent Trends in Canadian Corporate Governance." *Canadian Business Law Journal* 23: 23–44.

Kristol, I. 1978. *Two Cheers for Capitalism*. New York: Basic Books.

Linden, D.W. 1995. "Off with their Perks." *Forbes*, December 4.

LSE (London Stock Exchange). 1995. The Study Group on Directors' Remuneration (the Greenbury Committee). *Report.* London.

OSC (Ontario Securities Commission). 1995. "Staff Report on Executive Compensation and Indebtedness Disclosure." *Ontario Securities Commission Bulletin* 18, p. 666.

Waitzer, E.J. 1994. "Who's Afraid of Pay Disclosure?" *Ontario Securities Commission Bulletin* 17, p. 490.

Walters, A. 1995. "Let more earnings go to shareholders." *Wall Street Journal*, October 31, p. A23.

Yablon, C.M. 1992. "Overcompensating: The Corporate Lawyer and Executive Pay." *Columbia Law Review* 92 (November): 1867–1906.

Overhauling Executive Stock Options

Randall K. Morck

Hockey players, heiresses, and rock stars make most chief executive officers (CEOs) look decidedly middle class. Yet public clamor over CEO pay escalates. Although this concern may arise out of envy or ignorance, it is constructive. How CEOs are paid *is* more important than how hockey players, heiresses, or rock stars are paid. CEOs sit in the transmission of the economy — the others are hood ornaments.

How Capitalism Is Based on Trust

In a capitalist economy, people give money to managers in return for pieces of paper called shares and vague promises of unspecified future dividends. What is remarkable is that this system, based on trust and a veneer of law, actually works! Investors who buy shares usually get a fair return. If their trust in the financial system is seriously compromised, as it was in the 1930s, much of modern business grinds to a halt. Investors must trust corporate CEOs to act in their interests. Performance-based pay for top executives is, perhaps, a way to forge such trust: the CEO wins for himself when he wins for the shareholders.

How Corporate Decisions Can Go Wrong

If a CEO makes a decision that costs a company a million dollars, and the company has a million shareholders, each of them loses a

I am grateful for suggestions made by John McDougall and K. Hugessen.

dollar. If the manager owns a thousand shares, he loses a thousand dollars. But if the decision offers him personal benefits worth more than a thousand dollars, he may go ahead with it despite the cost to the firm.

Most CEOs are not self-interested money grubbers, but many critical business decisions are inherently uncertain. For example, hiring decisions almost always end up as judgment calls. Capital investment decisions are almost always based on incomplete data and forecasts rest on layers of assumptions; most companies quite sensibly use formal capital budgeting analyses only as inputs to these decisions with the final determinations depending on the business judgment of the top managers responsible.

People often convince themselves that what is best for them is also best for the world. Psychologists call this tendency cognitive dissonance. People try to frame the world in a way that is consistent with a good image of themselves. Thus, police officers genuinely believe the world would be better if they had more discretionary powers. Biologists honestly think biodiversity is essential to humanity's future. Professors are utterly convinced that tenure is essential to honest, open debate. Some political activists even describe patronage as a key part of any democratic political system — with no hint of mendacity in their voices!

These people may or may not be right, but it would be naive to think self-interest plays no role in forming their views. If self-interest colors peoples' view of the world, might top managers' self-interest bias their subjective judgment calls too?

Even if managers are completely unbiased, suboptimal decisions may still happen. Bureaucratic inertia can propel capital investment projects after their economic rationale has disappeared. Office politics can make silence an optimal policy for an ambitious, career-minded executive.

How This Is a Problem in the United States

Are these sorts of problems widespread enough to affect the overall economy? US financial analysts are increasingly convinced they are.

In the United States, most large firms are widely held, with their ownership divided among thousands of small shareholders. Managers there commonly have negligible equity stakes in their firms. Jensen and Murphy (1990b) report that the average CEO of a large US company owns 0.14 percent of its stock and the average CEO of a small one a hefty 0.49 percent.

A large and growing body of empirical results using US data points to a consistent pattern of substandard management in widely held firms. They have low market-to-book ratios and low earnings, and they make unprofitable acquisitions and diversify excessively. Firms in which managers own large blocks of stock or large outside stockholders exercise control over managers' decisions seem to do better[1] (although these firms may have other problems stemming from large shareholders' mistreatment of small shareholders). Combined with these results, the predominance of widely held firms in the United States points to a potentially serious public policy problem.

How Performance-Linked Pay for Top CEOs Is a Possible Solution

A solution to this problem is to link CEOs' self-interest to the performance of their firm, as it would be if they owned more stock in it (see Jensen and Murphy 1990a; 1990b). This reasoning underlies the various performance-based compensation packages many firms now offer top executives. If managers' wealth is linked to firm performance, we hope this may make them think harder about the consequences of their decisions. Prospective CEOs may also assess more carefully their chances of success. CEOs who secretly doubt they are up to the job will think harder about applying for it if their monetary reward is not guaranteed.

1 For evidence on these points, see Lewellen, Loderer, and Rosenfeld (1985); Tehranian et al. (1987); Morck, Shleifer, and Vishny (1988); Schmidt and Fowler (1990); and McConnell and Servaes (1990). Rose and Sheppard (1994) find that high average CEO pay is associated with other firm characteristics now associated with non-value-maximizing management, such as excess diversification and management entrenchment.

The effectiveness of pay-for-performance incentives is still an open question. If managers hype themselves into enthusiastically believing in a stupid project, cognitive dissonance might still swamp all coldly logical second thoughts. But if a stupid decision is driven ahead only by bureaucratic inertia or office politics, a pay-for-performance scheme may make a difference.

What Is the Track Record?

Do incentive-based compensation contracts work? The evidence is mixed. Brickley, Bhagat, and Lease (1985), Tehranian and Waegelein (1985), Lambert and Larcker (1985), and Waegelein (1988) find that share prices go up when firms announce pay-for-performance contracts with top managers. Yet Gaver, Battistel, and Battistel (1992) point out that share prices often rise when shareholder meetings are announced, and that pay for performance is often announced at the same time. DeFusco, Zorn, and Johnson (1991) find that the introduction of performance-based pay in US firms is actually followed by *worse* stock market performance and reduced research and development (R&D) spending. Leonard (1990) reports higher returns on equity in companies with long-term incentive plans. Waegelein (1988) documents increases in capital expenditures and no change in R&D spending. DeFusco, Johnson, and Zorn (1990) find that corporate risk taking seems to increase significantly after executive stock options are set up.

We do not know the answer mainly because existing pay-for-performance schemes are usually too weak to matter. Meaningful economic conclusions are consequently difficult. Lambert, Larcker, and Baker (1987) report that executive compensation is related to accounting earnings but not to share value. Kerr and Bettis (1987) find that top executive compensation is insensitive to stock price movements. Jensen and Murphy (1990a) present a detailed study of US executive compensation and conclude that "[i]n the majority of publicly held firms, the compensation of top executives is virtually independent of performance" and that the link between pay and performance is weaker now than it was in the 1930s. After examining the performance-pay and top-management incentives of more than 2,000 CEOs, Jensen and Murphy (1990b) find that, on average, their wealth changes $3.25 for every $1,000 change in shareholder wealth. Main (1991) finds a similar overall situation in the United Kingdom, and Elitzur and Halpern (1995) document the same for Canada.

The straight answer is that we think executive pay schemes *should* matter because there is overwhelming evidence that people do respond to monetary incentives. If these schemes are not working as they should, we should perhaps consider strengthening or changing the incentives they actually create. I believe that, in many cases, the incentives executives face from pay-for-performance plans are not only weak but also quite perverse. I shall explain why below.

Is This Relevant in Canada?

In the United States, CEO compensation schemes are one way of undoing perversions caused by wide ownership. Most Canadian companies are closely held; either the top managers themselves or an outside blockholder own dominant equity stakes (see Morck and Strangeland 1995).

If the CEO already owns large amounts of stocks, stock option plans and the like are redundant. Her wealth will not be more closely aligned with shareholders' interests if she is given a few stock options. Small shareholders' concerns here should focus on non-arm's-length transactions, self-dealing, and other problems that occur in closely held firms. Incentive-based CEO compensation is utterly irrelevant.

Many Canadian firms do have dominant shareholders who are not in charge on a day-to-day basis. Families with dominant equity stakes may hire professional managers to actually run the firm. In these cases, performance-based executive compensation schemes make sense. Indeed, Gomez-Mejia, Tosi, and Hinkin (1987) present evidence that pay for performance actually works best in such firms. Even in firms whose managers are also large shareholders, performance-based pay may make sense for lower-level executives.

A few Canadian firms are widely held. These include all the large chartered banks, both national airlines, and a few other very important companies. Although these firms make up a small percentage of the *Financial Post* 500, they are located in strategically important parts of the economy. Their performance is a key element of Canada's international competitiveness. Incentive-based compensation might well be a good idea in these companies.

Finally, the CEOs of public Canadian companies earn less than their US counterparts. A Towers Perrin 1991 survey of worldwide remuneration lists Canadian CEOs in companies with sales of about $250 million as earning an average of $407,600 annually in salary, bonuses, incentives, perquisites, and company contributions. In comparison, CEOs running similar companies in the United States earn about $747,500 (see Misutka 1992).[2] To attract and retain top-quality CEOs, Canadian firms must ante up competitive pay. Given Canada's national character flaw — a strait-laced and rather stuffy envy of success — that sort of compensation may ruffle public plumage. To avoid a dysfunctional "bonus envy" among the Canadian public, high executive pay should be clearly linked to outstanding performance.

Link CEO Pay to Share Prices, Not Earnings

Executive pay is often linked to the firm's accounting earnings, rather than its share prices (which are of more immediate concern to the typical investor). This approach is usually justified by alluding to shareholders' fixation on the short term, and consequent failure to appreciate the CEO's sagacity and providential insight. This is

2 A frequent response to this "pay gap" is that Japanese CEOs earn even less than Canadian CEOs, so all is well. That statement is probably false and certainly disingenuous. Although Japanese CEOs have relatively low salaries, Morck and Nakamura (1995) report Japanese firms' entertainment expenses that are similar in magnitude to their total R&D spending. If CEOs get even a small cut of these expenses, their actual remuneration may be quite high indeed. Regardless, good Canadian CEOs are more likely to move on to the United States than to Japan, so it is primarily US salaries that are relevant.

bunk for two reasons. First, earnings can be easily and legally manipulated. Second, there is no empirical evidence of shareholder myopia.

Earnings: CEOs as Short-Order Cooks

Linking CEO pay to current earnings, the quintessence of short-term performance, is probably not a clever way of inspiring long-term planning. At the very least, pay should be linked to average earnings over several years. Even this approach presents problems.

Earnings can be manipulated legally and without violating generally accepted accounting practice. Healy (1985) presents evidence that managers with earnings-linked bonus plans systematically manipulate accruals to increase earnings in years when upper limits on the bonuses are not binding and to reduce earnings in years when they are. Defeo, Lambert, and Larcker (1989) suggest that firms with earnings-based executive compensation organize equity-for-debt swaps to increase earnings by lowering interest payments, even when this increases corporate taxes.

In short, earnings are a myopic and sautéable measure of firm performance.

Options: Calling the Tune

Stock options reward managers when the share price rises. Share prices can be manipulated by timing the release of information and by releasing false information. The former action can, however, be interpreted as violating insider trading laws, and the latter is a felony. Overall, share prices are probably somewhat less subject to manipulation than earnings.

Market Myopia: Name Calling

Current share prices, despite claims to the contrary, reflect firms' *long-term* prospects. Hall (1990) finds higher market-to-book ratios, all else equal, when firms spend more on R&D. McConnell and

Muscarella (1985) report that share prices rise significantly when long-term investment projects are announced. Chan et al. (1990) find that share prices rise significantly when increases in R&D spending are announced. Markets may be inefficient in many ways, but they are not myopic. Shareholders clearly like firms that invest for the long term and rush to buy their shares. The myopic shareholder is a modern myth — like poodles in microwaves.

Managers are supposed to act in the interests of all their shareholders, but actual shareholder polls are cumbersome and expensive. Share prices give managers their only ongoing opinion poll of shareholders' views.

Dilution: Bluff Calling

If a firm pays its CEO with an option to buy at $30 and the share price rises to $40, his exercise of that option costs the firm $10. So the share price should fall by $10/*n*, where *n* is the number of shares outstanding. This share price decline, called dilution, that accompanies the exercising of executive stock options has been the subject of considerable furor in the popular press.

Dilution is not an illusion. Share prices do fall when new shares are sold at less than market value. The rub is that the same thing happens no matter how the firm pays its executives. If the CEO is paid $10 in excess salary, the cost to the firm is $10 too, and the price of every share falls by $10/*n* once again.

All CEO compensation costs the shareholders something. The issue is not dilution *per se*, but the overall level of compensation. If it is excessive, it hurts the shareholders, regardless of how it is paid. Concentrating on dilution makes little sense.

A Call for Change

Linking CEO pay to performance makes sense, and the best link available is stock options. Yet the use of stock options is increasingly being called into question. Many of the issues being raised, such as dilution and market myopia, are red herrings, but some concerns are nevertheless real.

Share prices can change for reasons utterly beyond managers' control. Options can provide perverse incentives toward risk taking. And despite insider trading laws, options can encourage self-interested timing of information releases. In contrast to the problems of earnings-based compensation, however, these problems can be readily contained by redesigning executive stock options slightly.

Putting Options in Context

Stock prices can go up or down just because interest rates change or for other reasons that are clearly not the manager's fault. If the share price movement is upward, the CEO wins big.[3] If it is downward, the board of directors usually just resets the options' strike price. For example, if the CEO received options to buy at the then-current share price of $30 and the share price falls to $15, the board often happily rewrites the options to let her buy at $15.

Some people allege that such adjustment is done whether the share price falloff resulted from the CEO's decisions or not.[4] The problem is that deciding what price movements are or are not the CEO's fault is very difficult. Asking the board to make this decision gives directors wide discretion and invites abuse.

Benchmarking: Performance Put to a Test

An alternative is to set up an *automatic* mechanism for adjusting the exercise prices of executive stock options. One way is to define that price in terms of an industry index. For example, suppose the share price of firm A is at $30, and the share prices of three rival firms in the same industry are $10, $5, and $100. Firm A's CEO can be given options to buy 100 shares for the value of 100 shares of rival firm B

3 This may be the real issue underlying outrage about dilution.

4 This may be why empirical links between CEO pay and firm performance are so tenuous despite the prevalence of executive stock option plans.

plus 200 shares of rival C plus 10 shares of rival D. The total now amounts to $3,000. If firm A's share price falls to $15 and the share prices of the rivals remain as they are, the CEO's options are worthless, as they should be. He is likely responsible for falloffs that affect only his firm. In contrast, if the price declines result from events beyond the CEO's control, they should affect the whole industry, and the prices of the three rivals' shares should also fall by 50 percent or so, reducing the value of 100 shares of rival B plus 200 shares of rival C plus 10 shares of rival D to $1,500. In this case, the CEO's options are still valuable. Where industry indexes exist, they can be used to define the exercise price. Diversified firms can use Toronto Stock Exchange indexes, such as the TSE 35 or TSE 300.

This approach essentially amounts to benchmarking the CEO's performance, a practice long used for portfolio managers. If a mutual fund earns 16 percent but the TSE 300 goes up 25 percent, the fund manager is likely to be fired. If the fund earns 10 percent when the market falls 30 percent, she is a hero. Where events beyond the actor's control can happen, what is important is relative, not absolute, performance.

Benchmarking means the directors need have no discretion to change the exercise price. The only choice they need make is the initial definition of that price. Which rival firms should this firm's performance be judged against?

Downside Risk: Striking a Balance

Most executive stock options are "at the money" when issued. If for example, the share price is $30 and the CEO gets options to buy at $30, he benefits personally if he can make the share price rise but has no cost if it falls. Such options create a perverse incentive to gamble. DeFusco, Johnson, and Zorn (1990) find that stock price variances rise after executive stock options are granted,[5] suggesting that the problem is more than an academic theory.

5 The same result appears to hold for both in-sample variance estimates and Black-Scholes implicit variance estimates derived from option prices.

How can this situation be remedied? The most straightforward way is to give the CEO options that are "in the money." For example, if the share price is at $30, he receives options to buy at $20; that way, his incentive to take imprudent risks is reined in by the possible loss of $10 that is now virtually in his pocket.

In-the-money options more accurately reproduce the effect on shareholders of managers' decisions. (Figure 1 illustrates.) If the share price remains at $30, the executive makes $10 buying at $20. If the share price rises to $40, he makes $10 more, for a total of $20 — the same increase the shareholder gains. If the share price falls to $20, the executive loses $10 and so does the shareholder.

In Canada, various regulatory and tax issues make this approach difficult. Firms can obtain the same result by paying executives with a combination of at-the-money options and restricted shares.[6] For example, three $20 options in the previous example are comparable to two $30 options and one restricted share.

By adjusting the mix of at-the-money options and shares, the board can fine tune the incentive to risk taking it creates. More at-the-money options mean the board wants a higher-risk strategy. More shares means that the board wants more attention paid to reducing risk.

European Options: An Exercise in Restraint

If an executive who owned only a sheaf of options in her own firm came to me for financial advice, I would tell her, Diversify! This advice is good for the executive, but it frustrates the purpose of the stock options: to link the executive's fortunes to the firm's share price.

How can the link be welded fast? A straightforward solution is to give executives European options, not the American options used

6 Restricted shares are usually treasury shares promised as future compensation if the executive remains with the firm long enough for them to vest — usually five years or so. Numerous variants of this approach are used in the United States.

Figure 1: *The Incentives Provided by Options*

Panel A: How at-the-money options reward CEOs when the stock price rises, but do not penalize them when it falls, thereby creating an incentive to gamble

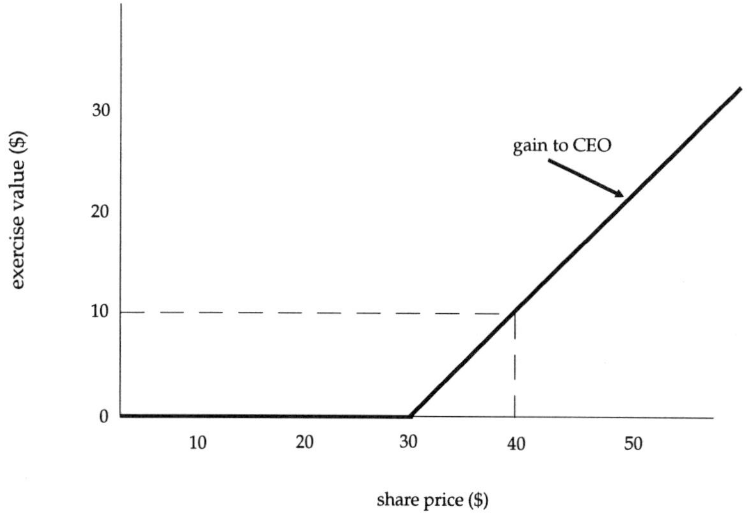

Panel B: How in-the-money options give CEOs incentives in tune with shareholders' interests

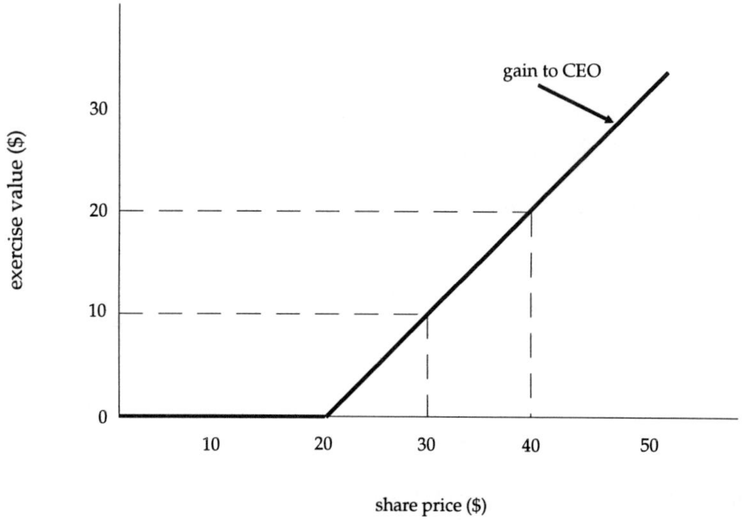

in Canada and the United States.[7] The exercise dates of European options and the vesting dates of restricted shares should both be set far enough in the future to tie the executive's fortune to the firm through her full term in office.

Unprincipled executives can time information releases to enhance the values of their stock options. For example, they may release positive information just before their options are to be exercised and save negative news for later. If blatant, this orchestration of information may raise concerns about insider trading, or even changes of stock price manipulation. Such accusations may, however, be difficult to prove. And small shareholders may not even realize they are being bilked.

European options can eliminate incentives to manipulate short-term share price movements, at least until the options mature. A firm should be required to publicly announce exercise dates for European executive stock options and vesting dates for restricted shares, both when they are issued and a few weeks before they expire and vest. Shareholders and securities commissions can thus be suspicious of "coincidental" news releases.

Putting the Public at Rest

Canadians have a stubborn egalitarian streak. They do not like people who get too rich too quickly. I believe this attitude to be self-destructive. If top executives at public companies cannot be paid competitively, other forms of business organization will displace public corporations.[8] The demise of public corporations would be unfortunate. They are a tangible link between democracy and capitalism. Shareholder democracy lets average Canadians participate in free enterprise. Replacing joint stock companies with less trans-

7 American options can be exercised any time up to their expiration date, European options can be exercised only *on* that date. In essence, European options do not *"vest"* until the day they expire.

8 Jensen (1989) argues that leveraged buyouts (LBOs) are an example. Since LBOs have no public shareholders, they can quietly give their executives radical pay-for-performance contracts that would evoke outrage from the press.

Table 1: *A Proposed Model for Disclosure of Executive Compensation*

	This Year	During 6 Years as CEO
Total salary and bonus	$200,000	$700,000
Value of options exercised	$12,000,000	$12,000,000
Net change in number of employees[a]	548	2,400
Net wealth created for shareholders[b]	$84,000,000	$197,000,000

[a] The changes represent a 6 percent increase in jobs this year and a 35 percent increase over six years. Other firms in the industry averaged 3 percent this year and 15 percent over the past six years.

[b] The changes represent a 17 percent return (dividends plus capital gains) this year and a 66 percent return over six years. Other firms in the industry averaged 15 percent this year and 45 percent over the past six years.

parent organizational forms would further concentrate economic power and ultimately erode public support for free enterprise.

Some business leaders rue the disclosure of executive compensation. They would hide from crypto-socialist censure, rather than refute it. Others try to deflect criticism, arguing that Canadian CEOs make less than their US counterparts. This response is true, but it misses the point,[9] and confounds the underlying problem of Canadians' purblind attitude toward success. If Canada is to compete in the global economy, we must have qualified people in charge of Canadian companies, and this costs money.

The only viable long-term strategy that might convince the Canadian public to support internationally competitive pay for top CEOs is to link that pay firmly and transparently to performance. CEOs who take home multimillion-dollar compensation must be seen to have created vast wealth for shareholders and many jobs for the nation. Accordingly, the disclosure of CEO pay should look something like Table 1.

9 See Misutka (1992) for the US-Canada comparison. Also, Jensen and Murphy (1990a) show that real CEO compensation in the United States has fallen since the 1930s; as a defense against critics of high CEO pay, this observation again misses the point.

Conclusion

I believe making the changes to executive options I suggest here and disclosing CEO pay in juxtaposition with information about performance will help dispel popular mythology of CEOs as inbred fat cats gorging on ill-got lucre. The onus is on boards to convince shareholders — and the public in general — that top executives are worth their pay. Otherwise, given Canadian politics and history, heavy-handed regulation or taxation is almost inevitable.

References

Brickley, J., S. Bhagat, and R. Lease. 1985. "The Impact of Long-Range Managerial Compensation Plans on Shareholder Wealth." *Journal of Accounting and Economics* 7 (1–3): 115–129.

Chan, S., et al. 1990. "Corporate R&D Expenditures and Share Value." *Journal of Financial Economics* 26 (3): 255–276.

Defeo, V.J., R.A. Lambert, and D.F. Larcker. 1989. "The Executive Compensation Effects of Equity-for-Debt Swaps." *Accounting Review* 64 (2): 201–227.

DeFusco, R.A. R.R. Johnson, and T.S. Zorn. 1990. "The Effect of Executive Stock Option Plans on Stockholders and Bondholders." *Journal of Finance* 45 (2): 617–627.

———, T.S. Zorn, and R.R. Johnson. 1991. "The Association between Executive Stock Option Plan Changes and Managerial Decision Making." *Financial Management* 20 (1): 36–43.

Elitzur, R., and P. Halpern. 1995. "Executive Compensation and Firm Value." In R. Daniels and R. Morck, eds., *Corporate Decision Making in Canada*. Calgary: University of Calgary Press.

Gaver, J.J., K.M. Battistel, and G.P. Battistel. 1992. "The Stock Market Reaction to Performance Plan Adoptions." *Accounting Review* 67 (1): 172–182.

Gomez-Mejia, L.R., H. Tosi, and T. Hinkin. 1987. "Managerial Control, Performance, and Executive Compensation." *Academy of Management Journal* 30 (1): 51–70.

Hall, B.H. 1990. "The Impact of Corporate Restructuring on Industrial Research and Development." *Brookings Papers on Economic Activity* (Microeconomics issue): 85–135.

Healy, P. 1985. "The Effect of Bonus Schemes on Accounting Decisions." *Journal of Accounting and Economics* 7 (1–3): 85–108.

Jensen, M.C. 1989. "Eclipse of the Public Corporation." *Harvard Business Review*, September-October, pp. 61–74.

———, and K.J. Murphy. 1990a. "CEO Incentives — It's Not How Much You Pay, but How." *Harvard Business Review*, May-June, pp. 138–149.

———, and K.J. Murphy. 1990b. "Performance Pay and Top-Management Incentives." *Journal of Political Economy* 98 (2): 225–264.

Kerr, J., and R.A. Bettis. 1987. "Boards of Directors, Top Management Compensation, and Shareholder Returns." *Academy of Management Journal* 30 (4): 645–664.

Lambert, R., and D.F. Larcker. 1985. "Golden Parachutes, Executive Decision-Making and Shareholder Wealth." *Journal of Accounting and Economics* 7 (1–3): 179–204.

———, D.F. Larcker, and G.P. Baker. 1987. "An Analysis of the Use of Accounting and Market Measures of Performance in Executive Compensation Contracts: Discussion." *Journal of Accounting Research* 25 (supplement): 85–129.

Leonard, J.S. 1990. "Executive Pay and Firm Performance." *Industrial and Labor Relations Review* 43 (February, special issue): 13-S–29-S.

Lewellen, C., C. Loderer, and A. Rosenfeld. 1985. "Merger Decisions and Executive Stock Ownership in Acquiring Firms." *Journal of Accounting and Economics* 7 (1–3): 203–232.

McConnell, J., and C. Muscarella. 1985. "Corporate Capital Expenditure Decisions and the Market Value of the Firm." *Journal of Financial Economics* 14 (September): 399–422.

———, and H. Servaes. 1990. "Additional Evidence on Equity Ownership and Corporate Value." *Journal of Financial Economics* 27 (October): 595–610.

Main, B.G.M. 1991. "Top Executive Pay and Performance." *Managerial and Decision Economics* 12 (3): 219–222.

Misutka, F. 1992. "Executive Compensation: The Biggest Headache Money Can Buy." *Canadian Business*, July, pp. 50–54.

Morck, R., and M. Nakamura. 1995. "Banks and Corporate Control in Japan." Unpublished manuscript.

———, A. Shleifer, and R. Vishny. 1988. "Management Ownership and Market Valuation: An Empirical Analysis." *Journal of Financial Economics* 20 (1): 293–316.

———, and D. Strangeland. 1995. "The Ownership of Canadian Firms." Unpublished manuscript.

Rose, N., and A. Sheppard. 1994. "Firm Diversification and CEO Compensation: Managerial Ability or Executive Entrenchment?" Massuchusetts Institute of Technology, Cambridge, Mass. Mimeographed.

Schmidt, D.R., and K.L. Fowler. 1990. "Post-Acquisition Financial Performance and Executive Compensation." *Strategic Management Journal* 11 (7): 559–569.

Tehranian, H., et al. 1987. "Management Compensation Contracts and Merger-Induced Abnormal Returns: Discussion." *Journal of Accounting Research* 25 (supplement): 51–84.

———, and J.F. Waegelein. 1985. "Market Reaction to Short-Term Executive Compensation Plan Adoptions." *Journal of Accounting and Economics* 7 (1–3): 131–144.

Waegelein, J.F. 1988. "The Association Between the Adoption of Short-Term Bonus Plans and Corporate Expenditures." *Journal of Accounting and Public Policy* 7 (1): 43–63.

Executive Compensation in Canada

Donald P. Lewis

Let me share with you some observations accumulated over 25 years of consulting on executive compensation, much of it focused on the relationship of executive pay to corporate performance.

The typical chief executive officer identifies totally with his or her company. Each CEO has a personal commitment that merges into the welfare of the business. Pay is, in part, an exchange for that commitment, but his or her perspective, as one might expect, is totally subjective. Pay has relatively little to do with a standard of living; it is primarily a scorecard to be compared with that of peers.

Directors, in particular those who serve on the committee that governs executive compensation, are somewhat more objective than the CEO, but they identify with the chief executive and want to be supportive. Acceptance of the scorecard concept diminishes the effectiveness of the committee, which should be focusing on performance, not comparability. More recent players in the pay issue are the institutional investors, who are completely objective, looking for a fair return over time in relation to risk.

Thus, this paper describes a straightforward methodology for measuring the relationship between pay and performance.

Pay and Performance

Let us begin with a definition of the two terms. *Pay* is total direct compensation (TDC), which is the sum of salary, bonuses, and other compensation and long-term pay (either in cash or stock option gains).[1] *Performance* is total return to shareholders (TRS) over the measurement period. It is based on the increase or decrease in share price plus dividends. In most circumstances, the optimum period of measurement is five years.[2]

Once TDC and TRS are calculated for a sample of firms, one can construct a chart showing their relative pay/performance relationships. It can apply to the CEOs only or to the firms' top five executive (including the CEOs); normally, both are prepared.

Figure 1 illustrates the situations of five companies. Company A has a high-pay/low-performance profile — the least desirable position. (The too-high pay may result from too-high salary, bonus, or stock options, or a combination.) Companies B and C have acceptable pay/performance profiles. Company D has a high-pay/high-performance profile, but the pay may be somewhat high relative to the peer group (perhaps it includes too many stock options). Company E has a low-pay/high-performance profile (a position that may result from maintaining one or more of the TDC components too low).

The chart is a snapshot in time. There is nothing to suggest that a company's relative position could not improve or decline in future periods, but continuing poor position should send a message to the board's compensation committee.

The Compensation Committee

We will return to considering the use of the chart, but first let us turn to the compensation committee, which is the focal point of corporate governance.

This committee, whose prime accountability is to the shareholders, should be composed of totally independent directors, with the definition of *independence* excluding individuals who supply

1 Retirement income may be a significant pay component, but it is omitted here because the measurement of the annual amount is contentious.

2 Because the disclosure regulations have been in effect for only two years, the maximum period of comparison until now has been four years. As companies report in 1996 for 1995, a five-year analysis will be possible.

Figure 1: *The Pay/Performance Profiles of Five Companies: A Matrix*

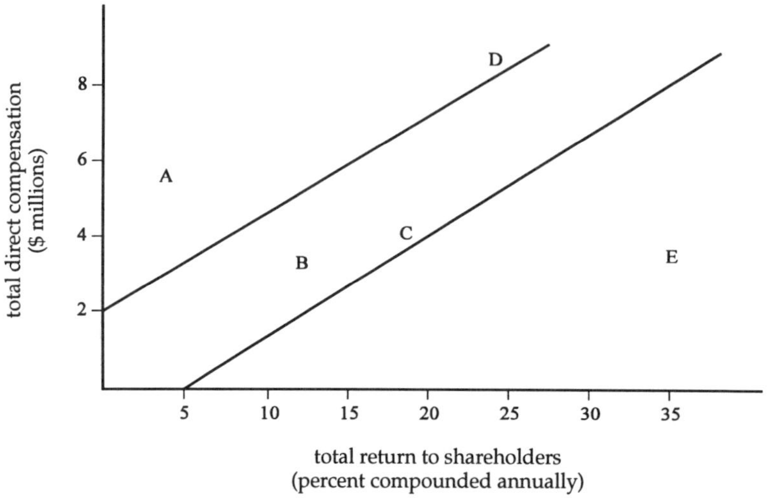

Note: To make the comparisons more valid, the TDCs have had a deflator applied according to company size.

services, such as legal counsel, to the company. The committee's point of departure should be setting goals for the percentage of total pay allocated to its fixed and variable components — salary, the annual bonus, and stock options.

Salary is the fixed component. How is it set? Often a committee states, in the company's annual information circular, that the salaries paid the CEO and other top executives are based on a survey (or surveys) and are intended to attract and retain the best people. The survey tends to be a self-fulfilling prophecy (in most cases, the sample is selected by management, rather than the committee). The number of executives at this level who move to another company in the same industry in Canada (or anywhere else for that matter) is virtually nil, and when a move occurs, salary is rarely an issue. Furthermore, the committee often positions salary at the 75th percentile of the sample group — higher than three-quarters of the others. The result is a steady increase, irrespective of the executive's performance or the company's ability to pay.

Annual bonus is one of the variable components of total pay. It is generally calculated on the basis of how well an executive meets one or more goals (which are normally quantifiable but, in a number of cases, subjective). The typical bonus is a percentage of salary if the individual attains a stated a target. The calculation yields zero for performance lower than a threshold, a nominal amount for performance between the threshold and the target, and a greater amount for performance above the target.[3] A number of weaknesses emerge from this typical approach to bonus determination:

- Linking the bonus to a salary creates pressure to maintain high salaries. A compensation committee that wants to increase the bonus component of total pay and reduce the salary component will uncouple the two.
- Too many compensation committees pay bonuses even when the amounts calculated are zero. They rationalize that the CEO and top executives worked very hard in a tough year and deserve something.
- Bonuses may be paid in a year when a company's share price has declined significantly. Such an action may be rationalized in the short term, but there should be consistency between bonuses and share price over a four- or five-year period.

Compensation analysts are developing better methods of measuring internal performance; economic value, for example, relates the return on invested capital to the cost of capital. The challenge in designing bonus plans is to keep the design simple enough to motivate participants while at the same time setting goals that are consistent with an increase in share price.

3 The calculation process is repeated when there is more than one goal.

Stock options, in many ways, are the ideal variable component of pay since the potential gain varies with increase in shareholder value. Perhaps the most critical element in the design has been the number granted. Too many dilutes the stock and gives the executive the opportunity for excessive gains; too few reduces the overall percentage of variable pay, placing too great an emphasis on fixed pay. The compensation committee must examine all issues pertaining to stock option grants and arrive at an allocation that is fair to shareholders and adequate to provide an incentive. In order to make the incentive long term, vesting should be delayed, permitting share price to attain a level supported by strategic decisions.

The Myth of the Market

Many executive compensation analysts claim that the market rules levels of pay, but my own research of pay practices among Canadian companies suggests that a number of those listed on the Toronto Stock Exchange (TSE) pay their top executives far in excess of the market, particularly in granting stock options. Furthermore, those executives' almost total absence of mobility from one company to another raises questions about the retention argument.

Relative to the United States, Canada has an abundance of larger companies controlled by an individual or a family. Usually, a prosperous private business becomes a listed public company but the family continues to hold a majority of the voting shares.[4] Among the TSE 35, family-controlled businesses with a family member as CEO include Rogers, Seagram, Thomson, Bombardier, and Power Corporation. Among other major Canadian public companies, the frequency of family control is evident. Such businesses often give family CEOs and top executives stock options far in excess of the typical grant. This action bears no relation to a market.

Mobility among middle- and lower-level executives is frequent as a vehicle to improve their careers and earnings. CEOs and top

4 There are also instances of families' exercising control with fewer than 50 percent of the voting shares.

executives, however, rarely move from company A to company B. When they do, the former employer is not a competitor with the new employer; for example, new CEOs at Moore, Laidlaw, Canadian Tire, and Nova did not work for competitors. Thus, the argument that high pay is needed to retain top executives is weak.

A better basis for determining executive compensation starts with the kind of analysis described above, comparing the company's pay/performance profile to the positions of one or more peer groups. As time proceeds, the compensation committee should analyze trends. That a company is consistently in the high-pay/low-performance part of the matrix should give the committee impetus to take whatever action is necessary. Institutional investors, not having the freedom to sell larger blocks of a poorly performing investment without disturbing the market, can discuss pay policies with compensation committees as part of an ongoing dialogue on corporate governance.

Conclusion

Many in society become emotional on learning that a top executive has earned $10 million, but the question from the compensation committee and from the institutional investor should be: Is the executive worth the payment? Although most people look to job earnings to provide funds for food, shelter, clothing, and other family expenditures, top executives earn far more than the amounts needed for a comfortable standard of living. They are motivated to earn more not to put bread on the table but as a measure of achievement.[5] Compensation of $10 million is meaningless in relation to personal consumption but may be significant in relation to the dollar increase in shareholder value.

The determination of executive pay is an art, not a science. Without being seduced by the numbers, the compensation committee has the accountability to pay top executives amounts that are justified by the total return to the shareholders over time.

5 In this context, executives are similar to professional athletes and entertainers.

In Conclusion

Closing Remarks

Thomas E. Kierans

To close this meeting, I will neither seek consensus nor delve into plumbing issues. Rather, I will proffer my own reflections on some of the larger issues raised today.

Disclosure

The first such issue is the appropriate scope for disclosure. As most of you in this room will recall, the notion of tabulating crime statistics by the racial origin of the perpetrator was deemed offensive in the late 1980s. Yet I recall the sociologist Raymond Breton telling me at the time that public information could be offensive only if it was wrong or incomplete. That, I think, is a key point. When Ed Waitzer said to Austin Beutel earlier today that half a loaf is better than no loaf, I thought he was wrong. Half a loaf is a bad deal, and getting to a whole loaf in terms of disclosure and full public information is what the game is all about.

I do argue, however, that the issue, although methodological, should not be regulatory. If information is, as I believe, a public good (because it enhances corporate efficiency and transparency), it is the responsibility of boards of directors to release all relevant data pertaining to executive remuneration and to outline their policies for determining compensation levels. Transparency and communications are not matters of boiler plate. I agree with Nick Ross. For a director sitting on a board compensation committee, having to sign each year a statement of how the committee compensates executives focuses the mind wonderfully. These are governance issues; they are not for the regulator. And enough rabbits have been set running in this game now that positive things are beginning to happen.

Indeed, I think we have convergence on one thing here today: there is no big role for regulators or legislators in policing compensation. The onus is now on markets, on proper disclosure, and on boards.

And in the area of governance, much has happened already. I am a big believer in happy interactions. I do not think the Toronto Stock Exchange's (TSE's) Dey Report made a big improvement *per se* in corporate governance. But it came at a time when corporate governance was about to undergo a big improvement in its own right. The combination of the two is really working. Corporate governance is not perfect yet, but it is evolving toward even higher standards of board performance.

Trust

There has been a lot of talk about trust today. I think there are three different "markets" for trust. The first is the trust of all the corporation's stakeholders, particularly its employees. With full disclosure, employees know the CEO's salary and bonus, and the policies informing remuneration. As a consequence, the CEO is forced, when working with the strategic business units, to push performance and incentive principles and extend them farther and farther down into the organization. This, I think, is a good thing. The second market for trust is external trust, which involves investors and the liquidity markets. And the third is trust in the market economy (Bob Brown has touched on that). The latter is crucially important. If anybody thinks it is not, just remember that Ottawa has the fiscal power to say that fixed executive compensation beyond a certain level will not be tax deductible for the corporation.

Short-Term and Long-Term Incentives

For rewarding CEOs and others, I reiterate the notion that "one size doesn't fit all." The matter is very complicated. First of all, I think directors must distinguish carefully between short-term incentives and long-term incentives. And short-term incentives have to be heavily weighed toward cash, if not entirely in it.

I commented this morning about economic value added versus economic value preserved. In a cyclical industry or in any industry strongly affected by exogenous factors, the reality is often that the best executives are the ones who cause the least harm to happen to the company over the short term, so it lives to fight another day. That consideration is crucial for short-term incentives. Now, industry benchmarks can easily be used to set short-term incentives. Sufficient data are published on return of capital employed, cash flow return on capital employed, and so forth. A deserving executive can be rewarded with a cash bonus, and an underperforming one punished by refusing to award it.

For the long term, however, firms should use some kind of stock-based scheme, if they can. (Some companies cannot, but others should do it wherever they can.)

Industry benchmarks play a part in both forms of compensation. Decisions should not be based just on whether a firm's shares have outperformed the TSE 300 or even competitors. Judgment weighs heavily in these matters.

Options and Executive Remuneration

One of the things that led to this conference today was my personal dissatisfaction with the way the TSE decided to allow firms to grant options in amounts greater than the previous cap of 10 percent of outstanding and issued common shares. Because that decision process lacked extensive consultation, it was not transparent enough for people to anticipate potential abuses. If you are going to do this kind of thing, you do not just drop it on the table.

But what's done is done. The effect is to put an enormous onus on boards of directors — on their governance decisions, on who is elected and who is re-elected (as Austin Beutel said earlier). It is going to create cumulative voting issues, which may result in shareholders' firing the entire MRCC if enough of them *perceive* abusive behavior. Heaven knows, there are abuses. Every industry has its key value-added drivers, complemented by senior executives who play significant but lesser roles. Today, in the aftermath of the TSE decision, some the latter are getting excessive annual option awards.

In brief, I have a problem with the TSE's options-granting decision, but it is no longer a regulatory matter. The regulators made an arbitrary decision and dumped the fair application of it in the laps of those responsible for governance — the directors.

Areas for Research

Setting executive remuneration is clearly a complex matter on which we need more research. Analysts in the United States have produced a considerable body of literature on the subject. But the academic community in Canada could do more work here for the benefit of Canadian practitioners and Canadian boards of directors.

One area in which we need study is how to separate the exogenous and endogenous factors that affect a firm's performance. As Will Mathews said earlier, "Stocks can go up if interest rates go down; therefore what has that to do with what the CEO should get?" In other words, how can we measure the CEO's actual value-added input as opposed to an apparently good share performance that could have happened anyway?

Some Canadians are starting to work on this matter — Randall Morck has provided us with an interesting approach to disclosure based on industry benchmarks — but academia could provide more guidance to boards.

Another item on a potential research agenda is supplementary executive retirement plans. They were not mentioned today (which surprises me), and they are not an item that must be disclosed. But they are common, they cost firms money, and executives presumably value them.

These plans have developed because the *Income Tax Act* permits a corporation to deduct for purposes of building a pension plan only amounts that create a final retirement income of no more than

$60,000 a year. That seems a small amount for a senior executive who is earning $700,000 or $1 million a year. So, of course, people have found ways around this limitation. A company simply enters into a contract with the executive to make ongoing retirement payments substantially in excess of the limit. If there is fear that the company may not honor the contract — say, because of a hostile takeover or bankruptcy — it can be backstopped by bank letters of credit, which cost the firm 0.0025 or 0.0050 percent a year and can be called upon by the executive at any time because they are long-term contractual commitments of the bank.

This kind of arrangement is not dealt with in any of the research I could find, and I would like to know what impact it has. If the six to ten people who make up a top management team are going to be able to retire at 60 or 70 percent of their best three or last three years' salaries for the rest of their lives, I want to know what effects this has on executives' risk appetites. Since the arrangement may well be part of negotiated termination settlements, it may well be a perverse incentive to excessive risk taking.

It is also another one of those tax issues that gets in the way of looking at appropriate compensation for all employees. If such schemes are available only to senior executives, are they right? They certainly distort the personal income tax system, the registered retirement savings plan system, and funded plan systems. In any event, analysts have not dealt with these schemes, and they should.

A third area of needed research is the use of the Black Scholes model for evaluating equity-based, long-term incentive grants. When I was an investment banker, I used to discount the theoretical values of warrants — or "haircut" them, in the jargon — when taking a financing package to market, even when they were fully and immediately liquid or detachable in 90 days. I would haircut them up to 50 percent as part of the pricing mechanism. I have not seen a good analysis of this practice for evaluating long-term equity incentives, which are normally illiquid.

Finally, we need to look at *directors'* options, with or without vesting. Here, I now disagree with what John McNeil said this morning. I, too, have always thought that directors served in a fiduciary capacity, and that they deserved directors' liability insurance and a variety of things like that, in addition to payment of a retainer and meeting fees, but that options were reserved to provide incentives to management.

Now, I learn that 35 percent of the companies listed on the TSE are awarding directors' options. The argument is that the directors should be aligned with shareholders to control management. This US practice is rolling like a tidal wave over Canada, but just because it is going on does not make it right. So we could probably use a bit more academic research on this subject.

Conclusion

Let me conclude by noting that, when Edward Iacobucci walked in here today, he got a hand because everybody thought he had done a superb paper. I thank him and Michael Trebilcock for their tremendous input, and Ed Waitzer for the Ontario Securities Commission's support for this conference. The best C.D. Howe Institute conferences are those that involve a meeting of academics and practitioners. They are enormously fruitful, and they do have an influence over time, whether they achieve consensus or not.

On behalf of the Institute, thank you very much for coming and participating.

The Contributors

James C. Baillie is Chair of the Executive Committee at Tory Tory DesLauriers & Binnington and a Director of Manulife Financial, FPI Inc., Midland Walwyn Inc., and The Standard Products Co. (USA). Apart from a period of just over two years (1978–80), when he served as Chairman of the Ontario Securities Commission, Mr. Baillie's career has been as a practising lawyer with Tory's. He now carries on a senior-level practice in the general area of business law. As one component of the practice, he frequently advises on corporate governance matters and represents independent committees of directors.

Austin C. Beutel co-founded Beutel Goodman and Company Limited, Investment Counsel, and retired from that firm in 1994. He is currently a private investor and serves on the boards of a number of public and private corporations. Mr. Beutel is a native of Montreal, and has a B. Comm. from McGill University and an M.B.A. from Harvard University.

Robert D. Brown is Chairman and Chief Executive Officer of Price Waterhouse, and has had a long and distinguished career in public accounting and examining the relationship of business to public policy and the total community. A graduate of the University of Toronto and the University of Chicago, Mr. Brown is a former Chairman of the Canadian Tax Foundation, a Director of the Council for Canadian Unity, a member of the Policy Board of the Business Council on National Issues, and First Vice Chair of the Canadian Institute of Chartered Accountants. He is a frequent contributor of articles to both popular and professional publications.

Martin F. Harts is the Partner in charge of the compensation group with KPMG, Actuarial, Benefits and Compensation Inc., which provides its clients with assistance on compensation advice and strategy, job evaluation, executive compensation, sales compensation, pay-for-performance, pay equity, employment equity, salary surveys, and employee performance management.

Edward Iacobucci is graduating in spring 1996 from the Faculty of Law, University of Toronto. He previously studied economics at Queen's University (B.A. Hons.) and Oxford University (M. Phil.), which he attended as a Rhodes Scholar. He has published papers on rent control policy and competition policy in Canada and Europe, respectively.

Thomas E. Kierans is President and Chief Executive Officer of the C.D. Howe Institute. A graduate of McGill University and the University of Chicago, he was President of McLeod Young Weir Limited (later ScotiaMcLeod Inc.) from 1979 to 1989, when he joined the Institute. He was also Chairman of the Energy Options Advisory Committee (to the federal government), the Ontario Economic Council, and the Royal Ontario Museum. Mr. Kierans is currently Chairman of First Marathon Securities Limited and Petro-Canada, and serves as a Director of Ipsco Inc., Inmet Mining Corporation, The Manufacturers Life Insurance Company, TransCanada PipeLines, and several other privately owned Canadian companies.

Donald P. Lewis has been a management consultant specialist in executive compensation for more than 25 years. He was a partner in two international consulting firms for 20 years; in 1994, he retired, formed his own firm, and developed an in-depth executive compensation analysis service. Mr. Lewis has co-authored a number of studies in executive compensation with the National Centre for Management Research and Development at the University of Western Ontario.

Jeffrey G. MacIntosh is Professor of Law in the Faculty of Law at the University of Toronto. He has published widely in the area of corporate and securities law on such topics as shareholders' rights, the legal relationship between majority and minority shareholders, corporate takeovers, poison pills, the statutory oppression remedy, appraisal rights, the role of institutional and retail investors in Canadian capital markets, and directors' fiduciary duties. His current research deals with the special problems of financing small firms in Canada, with a focus on venture capital and initial public offerings. Professor MacIntosh currently sits on the Ontario Securities Commission Task Force on Small Business Financing. In 1988–89, he served as John M. Olin Fellow in Law and Economics at the Yale Law School.

John D. McNeil is Chairman and Chief Executive Officer, Sun Life Assurance Company of Canada. A graduate of the University of Edinburgh (M.A., Honours in Political Economy), Mr. McNeil originally joined Sun Life in 1956, but left in 1966 to pursue a career in mutual funds mangement. He rejoined Sun Life in 1979, and assumed his current position in 1988. Mr. McNeil is a Director of a number of companies, including Canadian Pacific Limited and Shell Canada Limited; he is also a Director and former Chairman of the C.D. Howe Institute, and a member of the Business Council on National Issues and the Ontario Business Advisory Council.

Randall K. Morck is Professor of Finance and holder of the Stephen A. Jarislowsky Distinguished Chair in Finance at the University of Alberta. Dr. Morck graduated *summa cum laude* from Yale University in 1979 with a B.Sc. in Applied Mathematics and an M.A. in Economics. He obtained a Ph.D. in Economics from Harvard University in 1986. He has published extensively on issues relating to corporate finance, corporate governance, and international corporate finance, and is a frequent speaker at academic meetings, university workshops, and business seminars.

Michael J. Trebilcock is Professor of Law, Director of the Law and Economics Programme, and Chairman of the International Business and Law Programme at the University of Toronto. Among his recent publications are *Unfinished Business: Reforming Trade Remedy Laws in North America* (1993); *The Prospects for Reinventing Government* (1994); and *Getting There: An Assessment of the Agreement on Internal Trade* (edited, with Daniel Schwanen, 1995), all of which were published by the C.D. Howe Institute.

Edward J. Waitzer is Chairman of the Ontario Securities Commission. He received his LL.B. and LL.M. degrees from the Faculty of Law, University of Toronto, and from 1977 to 1981 he worked for the Toronto Stock Exchange as Vice-President, Listings and Distributions. Thereafter, he was a Partner of Stikeman, Elliott in their Toronto and New York offices until joining the Commission in November 1993. He has written extensively on a variety of legal and public policy issues, and has served as a director of a number of corporations and community organizations.

Adam H. Zimmerman is the retired Chairman and former Chief Executive Officer of Noranda Forest Inc. and other companies. He is Director of several companies, including MacMillan Bloedel Limited, Southam Inc., and the Toronto-Dominion Bank. He has been active in community affairs as a Trustee of the Hospital for Sick Children, Deputy Chairman of the University of Toronto Breakthrough Campaign, and, currently, Chairman of the Commonwealth Games Club. He is also a former Chairman of the C.D. Howe Institute. A graduate of the Royal Canadian College and the University of Toronto, Mr. Zimmerman was appointed an Officer of the Order of Canada in 1994.

Members of the C.D. Howe Institute*

* The views expressed in this publication are those of the authors and do not necessarily reflect the opinions of the Institute's members.

Cogeco inc.
Consoltex Group Inc.
Consumers Gas
Coopers & Lybrand
Dr. Glen H. Copplestone
E. Kendall Cork
William J. Cosgrove
Co-Steel Inc.
Marcel Côté
Pierre Côté
John Crispo
Glen E. Cronkwright
Devon Gaffney Cross
John Crow
Crown Life Insurance Company Limited
Paul R. Curley
Thomas P. d'Aquino
Leo de Bever
W. Ross DeGeer
Catherine Delaney
Deloitte & Touche
Desjardins Ducharme Stein Monast
Robert Després
Deutsche Bank Canada
Iain St. C. Dobson
The Dominion of Canada General Insurance Company
DuPont Canada Inc.
Gordon H. Eberts
Edper Group Limited
Emerging Markets Advisors Inc.
The Empire Life Insurance Company
ENSIS Corporation
Ernst & Young
Export Development Corporation
Ronald J. Farano, Q.C.
First Marathon Securities Limited
Aaron M. Fish
John P. Fisher
Fishery Products International Limited
C.J. Michael Flavell, Q.C.
Ford Motor Company of Canada, Limited
Formula Growth Limited
L. Yves Fortier, C.C., Q.C.
Four Seasons Hotels Limited
GSW Inc.
Jim Garrow
General Electric Canada Inc.
General Motors of Canada Limited
Joseph F. Gill
Gluskin Sheff + Associates Inc.
Goldman Sachs Canada
Goodman Phillips & Vineberg
Peter Goring
Dr. John A.G. Grant
Dr. Jerry Gray
The Great-West Life Assurance Company
Greyhound Lines of Canada
Morton Gross
Le Groupe Canam Manac
Groupe Sobeco Inc.
Dr. Geoffrey E. Hale
H. Anthony Hampson
C.M. Harding Foundation
Brian Harrison
G.R. Heffernan
Lawrence L. Herman
Hewlett-Packard (Canada) Ltd.
Gordon J. Homer
Honeywell Limited
Hongkong Bank of Canada
The Horsham Corporation
Dezsö Horváth
H. Douglas Hunter
Lou Hyndman, Q.C.
IBM Canada Ltd.
Imasco Limited
Imperial Oil Limited
Inco Limited
Inland Cement Limited
The Insurance Bureau of Canada
Interprovincial Pipe Line Inc.
Investment Dealers Association of Canada
The Investment Funds Institute of Canada
Investors Group Inc.
IPSCO Inc.
Tsutomu Iwasaki
The Jarislowsky Foundation
KPMG
Mark D. Kassirer
Joseph Kruger II
Jacques A. Lefebvre
Gérard Limoges
Loewen, Ondaatje, McCutcheon Limited

London Life Insurance Company
J.W. (Wes) MacAleer
McCallum Hill Companies
McCarthy Tétrault
W.A. Macdonald
Bruce M. McKay
McKinsey & Company
Maclab Enterprises
James Maclaren Industries Inc.
Jack M. MacLeod
McMillan Binch
MacMillan Bloedel Limited
William J. McNally
Mannville Oil & Gas Ltd.
Manulife Financial
Maple Leaf Foods Inc.
Dr. Georg Marais
Marsh & McLennan Limited
Hon. Dwight N. Mason
Master Equity Investments Inc.
James Mauldin
The Mercantile and General Reinsurance Group
William M. Mercer Limited
Merck Frosst Canada Inc.
Methanex Corporation
Metropolitan Life Insurance Company
Robert Mitchell Inc.
The Molson Companies Limited
Monsanto Canada Inc.
The Montreal Exchange
Montreal Trust
Moore Corporation Limited
Morgan Stanley Canada Inc.
Hugh C. Morris, Q.C.
Munich Reinsurance Company of Canada
The Mutual Life Assurance Company of Canada
National Trust
Nesbitt Burns
E.P. Neufeld
Newcourt Credit Group Inc.
Noma Industries Limited
Noranda Forest Inc.
Noranda Inc.
Northwood Pulp and Timber Limited
NOVA Corporation
Onex Corporation
Ontario Hydro
The Oshawa Group Limited
Katsuhiko Otaki
James S. Palmer
PanCanadian Petroleum Limited
Pembina Corporation
Petro-Canada
Philips, Hager & North Investment Management Ltd.
Pirie Foundation
Les Placements T.A.L. Ltée.
Placer Dome Inc.
Frank Potter
Patricia Pouliquen
Power Corporation of Canada
Pratt & Whitney Canada Inc.
Price Waterhouse
J. Robert S. Prichard
Procor Limited
ProGas Limited
QUNO Corporation
RBC Dominion Securities Inc.
Redpath Industries Limited
Henri Remmer
Retail Council of Canada
Richardson Greenshields of Canada Limited
R.T. Riley
Gordon Ritchie
Robin Hood Multifoods Inc.
Rogers Communications Inc.
J. Nicholas Ross, C.A.
Rothschild Canada Limited
Royal Bank of Canada
ROYCO Hotels & Resorts
SNC Lavalin Group Inc.
St. Lawrence Cement Inc.
Samuel, Son & Co., Limited
Sandwell Inc.
Sanpalo Investments Corporation
Guylaine Saucier
André Saumier
Sceptre Investment Counsel
Sceptre Resources Limited
Dick Schmeelk
ScotiaMcLeod Inc.

Shirley B. Seward
Sharwood and Company
Shell Canada Limited
Sidbec-Dosco (Ispat) Inc.
Sierra Systems Consultants Inc.
Southam Inc.
Spar Aerospace Limited
Speirs Consultants Inc.
Philip Spencer, Q.C.
The Standard Life Assurance Company
Stelco Inc.
Sun Life Assurance Company of Canada
Suncor Inc.
Swiss Re Life Canada
TELUS Corporation
Laurent Thibault
Thornmark Corporation
3M Canada Inc.
The Toronto Dominion Bank
The Toronto Stock Exchange
Torstar Corporation
Tory Tory DesLauriers & Binnington
TransAlta Utilities Corporation
TransCanada PipeLines Limited
Trimac Limited
Trizec Corporation Ltd.
Robert J. Turner
Unilever Canada Limited
United Grain Growers Limited
Urgel Bourgie Limitée
Vancouver Stock Exchange
VIA Rail Canada Inc.
Viridian Inc.
J.H. Warren
West Fraser Timber Co. Ltd.
Westcoast Energy Inc.
Weston Forest Corporation
Alfred G. Wirth
M.K. Wong & Associates Ltd.
Fred R. Wright
Xerox Canada Inc.
Paul H. Ziff

Honorary Members

G. Arnold Hart
David Kirk
Paul H. Leman
J. Ross Tolmie, Q.C.